THE KING'S SERVICE

Miss Josephine Silverwood

THE CORONATION

Dr Randall Davidson, Archbishop of Canterbury, setting St Edward's Crown upon the head of King George V in Westminster Abbey, June 22, 1911. The King is wearing the priestly stole and dalmatic, and holding the sceptre in one hand and the rod with the dove in the other.

Photo Graphic Photo Union

THE KING'S SERVICE

By

M. C. CAREY

AUTHOR OF "PRINCESS MARY" ETC.

and

DOROTHY MARGARET STUART

AUTHOR OF "THE BOY THROUGH THE AGES" ETC.

GEORGE G. HARRAP & CO. LTD.

In conjunction with

THE JUNIOR BOOK CLUB LTD.

Dedicated

BY THE GRACIOUS PERMISSION

OF

THE KING

TO

His Majesty's
Grandchildren

First published 1935
by GEORGE G. HARRAP & CO. LTD.
182 High Holborn, London, W.C.1

Copyright.   All rights reserved

———————————————

Made in Great Britain.   Printed by Morrison & Gibb Ltd.
London and Edinburgh

The centre of all this pomp and pageantry was a little old lady with a black bonnet trimmed with a tuft of white plumes, dressed in a robe of black-and-white lace, and carrying a sunshade. Some onlookers thought that Queen Victoria was almost dazed by the warmth of the welcome her people gave her, but her own diary proves that she was keenly observant of everything, and intensely responsive to the affection that she inspired.

Hers was a very different England from the England which celebrates the twenty-fifth year of her grandson's reign. The horse-bus and the hansom were then in undisputed possession of our streets ; wireless was not yet thought of ; the cinema was a new toy, a silent spectacle of flickers and flashes ; the gramophone, another new toy, had begun to astonish people by emitting harsh squeals which resembled recognizable voices or melodies. The motor-car was an unfamiliar and uncouth object, seeing which astonished horses would plunge and rear. Heavier-than-air flying-machines had not got beyond the earliest experimental stage in 1897 ; radium had not been discovered ; all the Great Powers of Europe were monarchies, with the exception of France.

Only thirty-eight years have passed since the bells of London rang joyous peals in honour of Victoria, Queen and Empress, and mother of her people. In many ways they have been years of dazzlingly rapid progress and wildly unforeseen developments. But in other ways they have seen few changes in the fabric of the English national life, deep-rooted in the character of the people, and expressing itself still in symbols as ancient as the Stone of Destiny on which so many kings have been crowned. The King still stands at the summit and at the centre of our constitution, as head of our political, social, and civic system. Upon his personality, and upon the use he makes of his unique opportunities, the future of our race depends as much as upon any other single factor in the British Commonwealth to-day. To set forth and interpret some of the ancient symbols of kingship, and to trace some of the characteristics and activities of the King, is the object of this book.

An uninterrupted reign of twenty-five years may not mean that peace has been unbroken and progress uninterrupted for the whole of that time ; but it usually indicates a period of stability, unmarked by sudden catastrophes or fierce upheavals, a period during which advances have been made, and victories won, in various fields of national activity. This is especially true of the Jubilees celebrated by Queen Victoria in 1887 and 1897, the fiftieth and sixtieth anniversaries of her accession, and, in spite of grave events both at home and abroad, it is true of the Jubilee celebrated this year by her grandson, King George V. Hers was the longest reign in English history—four years longer than that of her grandfather, George III. Other long reigns have been those of Henry III (1216–1272), Edward III (1327–1377), Henry VIII (1509–1547), and Elizabeth (1558–1603).

All these epochs were both memorable and interesting. Under Henry III, Parliament came into being, and many of our great English Abbeys and Cathedrals were built ; under Edward III we won brilliant victories in France, and our literature began to take shape ; under Henry VIII, England felt the double impulse of the Renaissance and the Reformation ; under Elizabeth she reached the peak of her intellectual glory. The closing years of George III's reign were rendered perilous and exciting by the last stages of the struggle with Napoleon, but this, too, was a period of progress—scientific, literary, and political—and it prepared the way for more steady and solid developments under Victoria.

Let us take a backward glance at the Jubilee of 1897, the last Jubilee celebrated in London, for King George's father, Edward VII, had a comparatively brief reign of nine years. Cheering throngs acclaimed the aged Queen when she drove through the gaily-decorated streets to the thanksgiving service in St Paul's.

> Here were Hausas from the Niger and the Gold Coast, coloured men from the West India regiments, Zaptiehs from Cyprus, Chinamen from Hong-Kong, and Dyaks from British North Borneo ; here were Englishmen, Scotsmen, Irishmen, and Welshmen, Imperial Service troops sent by the native princes of India, and a detachment of Sikhs.[1]

---

[1] Clare Jerrold, *The Widowhood of Queen Victoria.*

FOREWORD

DURING the present year of grace, 1935, the word 'Jubilee' will constantly be heard throughout the British Commonwealth of Nations in connexion with the rejoicings which mark the twenty-fifth anniversary of King George's accession to the Throne. The history of this word is full of the colour and glamour of the distant past, and it forms one of those invisible but very strong bridges linking our civilization with the vanished world of antiquity.

In Latin, *jubilare* meant 'to exult with shouts of joy'; but learned men trace 'Jubilee' to another and yet more ancient language—to Hebrew, in which *yobel* meant a ram's horn, such a horn as was blown at certain Jewish festivals. It was from the Jewish religion that the Christian Church took both the name and the idea of the *Annus Jubilæus*, or year of rejoicing. Pope Boniface VIII decided that 1300 should be such a year, and thousands of pious people flocked to Rome to share in the celebrations. A later pontiff decided to proclaim a Jubilee every fifty years, and later still this term was halved, and every twenty-five years was the appointed period of rejoicing. These were, of course, purely religious Jubilees. The idea is an apparently recent one in connexion with non-religious anniversaries.

It may be—and probably will be—asked, "Why should a country regard it as a cause for rejoicing that the same Sovereign has reigned for twenty-five, or for fifty, years?" There are several good answers to that quite natural question. In the first place, frequent changes upon the Throne are always historically unfortunate. If the change was caused by rebellion or civil war, there must have been violence, damage, and suffering from which no section of the people could escape. If the untimely death of the King were the cause, that meant a long minority, with all its attendant evils : for, as Langland remarked when the boy-King Richard II wore the crown,

Where the cat is a kitten
The land is lawless.

6

To the Boys and Girls of the Borough of Barnes

HIS Majesty King George V has reigned for twenty-five years, and this is the reason that we are all celebrating his Majesty's Silver Jubilee this year.

I ask you to study carefully the life of his Majesty, and his unbounded devotion to the cause of his subjects.

You cannot do better than follow the lead he has set. By so doing you will adequately fit yourselves to take a useful part in the maintenance of our nation's well-being.

His Majesty is a great sportsman. Follow, therefore, his example and always 'play the game,' in order that you may, in your generation, become useful and honourable citizens.

Jubilees, marking long reigns and the nation's respect and affection for its monarch, are not frequent, and I hope you will remember to-day as a happy event as well as a milestone in this country's glorious history.

Percy Hamilton Hughes.

MAYOR

6th May, 1935

CONTENTS

I

TRADITION AND PRIVILEGE

By

DOROTHY MARGARET STUART

THE KING AND QUEEN AT DELHI IN THEIR CORONATION ROBES, 1911–12

Photo Central Press

ST EDWARD'S CROWN, USED IN THE ACTUAL
CORONATION CEREMONY

THE ROYAL SCEPTRE, LARGER ORB
AND QUEEN'S SCEPTRE

THE AMPULLA, IN WHICH THE ANOINTING OIL
IS HELD

THE IMPERIAL CROWN, SHOWING THE
BLACK PRINCE'S RUBY

Photo Sport and General

I

TRADITION AND PRIVILEGE

The Crowning of the King

WHEN King Edward VII, the father of King George V, died, after a very brief illness, in May 1910, one of the first things that happened was that a squadron of Life Guards prepared to turn out, if necessary, in five minutes from the trumpet-call, to suppress any sudden rebellion. This quaint custom was a heritage from more troublous times, when the death of the Sovereign was quite likely to produce tumults. For the same reason, English kings used in the old days to spend the night before the Coronation within the sheltering walls of the Tower.

The next thing that happened, on the very day following King Edward's death, was the solemn Proclamation of his son. Standing in the Friary Court of the Palace of St James's, Garter King-of-Arms, arrayed in his richly coloured heraldic tabard and announced by a double fanfare on the silver trumpets of the even more gorgeous State Trumpeters, read in a clear voice the Proclamation beginning, " Whereas it has pleased Almighty God to call to His mercy our late Sovereign Lord King Edward the Seventh of Blessed and Glorious Memory," and declaring that

> We, therefore, the Lords Spiritual and Temporal of this Realm, being here assisted with those of his late Majesty's Privy Council, with numbers of other principal gentlemen of quality, do now hereby with one voice and consent of tongue and heart proclaim
>
> That the High and Mighty Prince George Frederick Ernest Albert is now, by the death of our late Sovereign of Happy Memory, our only lawful and rightful Liege Lord.

15

From the garden wall of their home, Marlborough House, the new King's only daughter, and three of his sons, watched the ancient ceremony with interest ; the two elder boys, wearing the uniform of naval cadets, standing rigidly at the salute when the crowd echoed the Herald's solemn *God Save the King*. Everything passed off quietly. The Life Guards had no tumults to quell.

Preparations for the crowning of a British King are necessarily very complicated, especially as he is also King of the British Dominions beyond the Seas and Emperor of India. King George was not crowned until June 22, 1911, more than a year after his accession, and many people had been working hard during the intervening months to prepare the splendours of his Coronation.

The Crown Jewels

What happens when the King receives crown, sceptre, and orb before the High Altar of the Abbey of Westminster ? One of the things that happens is that the long-dead past comes suddenly to life again. Much of the ceremony dates back to Biblical days, when Samuel anointed Saul, and when Zadok the Priest anointed Solomon, King over Israel. In very distant times, among the tribes of northern Europe, the newly elected King had to stand on a shield which was then lifted on the shoulders of four of the stoutest of his warriors and carried among the assembled people. Later kings may well be thankful that this ordeal does not form part of *their* coronation ceremony ! The *corona* was first of all a triumphal wreath of green foliage ; then it developed into a woven diadem ; then into a flexible fillet of gold ; and, by way of a golden circlet, it became the arched and jewelled crown familiar to us to-day.

Most of us know that the Regalia, the Crown Jewels of England, are now kept behind strong iron bars in the Tower of London, but from the time of Edward the Confessor to that of Charles II

THE KING AND QUEEN IN THE STATE COACH AT THEIR CORONATION, 1911

Photo Sport and General

THE KING AT TEMPLE BAR, THE WESTWARD BOUNDARY OF THE CITY OF LONDON

In accordance with the ancient custom he touches the pearl-handled City sword proffered by the Lord Mayor.
Notice the fur hat of the sword-bearer, another relic of the past.

b

Photo Central Press

THE KING ON HIS WAY TO THE TROOPING OF THE COLOUR
A military ceremony dating from the time of Charles II.
Photo Sport and General

THE RETURN FROM THE TROOPING OF THE COLOUR
The King at the head of his Guards.
Photo J. Dixon Scott

they were lodged in the grim, gloomy Chapel of the Pyx at Westminster. Before the Civil War they included many marvellous historical relics—King Alfred's crown and Moses' wand among them. The Cromwellians, however, laid violent hands upon these national treasures, and had them broken up and sold for small sums. Happier was the fate of the Scottish Regalia, hidden for many years beneath the pavement of the lonely little church of Knieff!

A brand-new crown had to be made for Charles II, " when the King enjoyed his own again," but some of the age-old jewels of the ancient Regalia are still to be seen in our present King's great State crown, among them the " fair ruby " given by Pedro the Cruel to the Black Prince and worn by Henry V on his helmet at the battle of Agincourt. All these Royal jewels, with the Queen Consort's crown, St Edward's crown, two orbs, five sceptres, four swords, and the golden Ampulla (or eagle) to hold the sacring oil, are taken from the Tower to Westminster on the eve of the Coronation, and guarded all night in the dim, tapestry-hung apartment known as the Jerusalem Chamber.

On June 22, 1911, a vast throng of subjects, noble and simple, gathered in the grey Abbey to do homage to their " only lawful and rightful Liege Lord " ; peers and peeresses in their deep red robes trimmed with miniver ; archbishops and bishops in shimmering copes, or with snowy, billowing sleeves of lawn ; foreign royalties in a bewildering variety of gorgeous uniforms ; Privy Councillors and Elder Brothers of Trinity House looking like naval officers in their uniforms of dark blue and gold ; Indian princes in turbans hued like a bed of tulips. King George was first seen wearing a crimson robe with a deep ermine cape, and a cap edged with ermine ; Queen Mary's gown was of white satin, embroidered with gold, and her trailing mantle was of deep purple velvet thickly encrusted with Royal and Imperial emblems worked in heavy gold thread.

2

The actual ceremony began when the Archbishop of Canterbury, Dr Randall Davidson, presented the King four separate times to the people, at each of the four points of the compass, with these words :

> Sirs, I here present to you King George, the Undoubted King of this Realm. Wherefore all you who are come this day to do your Homage and Service are you willing to do the Same ?

The people, led by the shrill, triumphant voices of the Westminster schoolboys, cried loudly, *God Save the King !*

The Regalia had now been placed upon the High Altar, and the Holy Communion service, of which the Coronation is part, proceeded. After the sermon, by the Archbishop of York, the Archbishop of Canterbury administered to the still uncrowned King a solemn threefold oath that he would govern " according to the statutes in Parliament agreed on," cause " Law and Justice in Mercy to be executed," and " maintain and preserve the Church of England." Bareheaded and kneeling he received the Sacrament. Then, after Handel's impressive anthem " Zadok the Priest " had been sung, the King's red robes were taken from him, and he seated himself in the battered wooden chair first used at the coronation of Edward II—the chair beneath which is the immemorially ancient Stone of Destiny brought from Scotland by Longshanks, a greater Edward and first of that illustrious name.

The Anointing

Now came that part of the ceremony always regarded as the most solemn—the anointing.

> Not all the water in the rude, rough sea
> Can wash the balm from an anointed King.

So says Shakespeare's Richard II, and in saying this he did but express a common and long-cherished belief.

The Archbishop poured some of the oil from the Ampulla

into a golden spoon, and anointed the King's head, uttering these words, " Be thy head anointed with holy oil, as kings, priests, and prophets were anointed." The King's breast and the palms of both his hands were anointed next, and he was vested in a linen robe, then in a supertunica, or dalmatic, of cloth of gold. Still seated, he received the sword and the spurs—the former being offered up at the altar and ' redeemed ' for one hundred shillings. It is the duty of the Dean of Westminster to place round the King's neck the ' Armill ' or golden stole and to invest him in his Imperial mantle of purple lined with ermine. As Lord of the Manor of Worksop, the Duke of Newcastle then presented him with an embroidered glove, according to a custom which dates from the Norman Conquest, and the Archbishop presented him with the orb, the emblem once of Roman authority over the whole globe ; next he received the sceptre, symbol of kingly power, and the rod with the dove, symbol of equity and mercy.

The Dean at this point brought from the altar the crown of St Edward, which the Archbishop set upon the King's head. It is always the Archbishop of Canterbury who, on behalf of the Peers Spiritual, is the first to do homage to the newly crowned King. The Prince of Wales, a slim, boyish figure in the robes of a Knight of the Garter, was the first to do homage on behalf of the princes of the blood royal. He affirmed his allegiance to his father in this time-honoured formula :

> I, Edward, Prince of Wales, do become your liege man of life and limb, and of earthly worship : and faith and truth will I bear unto you to live and die, against all manner of folks, so help me God.

One peer of each Order, that is to say, one Duke, one Marquis, one Earl, one Viscount, and one Baron, in turn did homage on behalf of all his fellow-peers of the same rank, who doffed their coronets in unison with him, when he promised to support the Crown " with all his power."

Queen Mary was anointed on the head only, and crowned with a crown made especially for the occasion, set in the centre with the famous Koh-i-noor (Mountain of Light) diamond. "Receive the crown of glory, and of honour, and of joy," said the prelate who set it upon her forehead. Four peeresses held a rich canopy over her during this part of the ceremony.

Now the order of the Communion Service, interrupted for a time, is resumed, and the King makes oblation of bread, wine, an altar-cloth, and an ingot of gold. Then, while the *Te Deum* was being sung, their Majesties withdrew to robing-rooms prepared for them behind the High Altar, where the King exchanged St Edward's crown for his Imperial crown, and whence he emerged wearing his purple robe, and carrying the sceptre in his right and the orb in his left hand. Then, down the whole length of the nave he walked, the Barons of the Cinque Ports carrying over his head a golden canopy with a silver-gilt bell at each corner, and all the peers following with their coronets on their heads and their crimson mantles trailing behind them.

Four swords are borne by four peers before the King on this great occasion; the 'Curtana,' or pointless sword of mercy, the sword of offering, the sword of spiritual justice, and the sword of temporal justice. Each gold spur is carried by an earl, and the Duke of Northumberland, as Lord High Steward of England, carries the King's crown.

Early in the nineteenth century the custom of the Coronation banquet in Westminster Hall was abandoned, and with it the ancient ceremony of the King's Champion, who used to ride into the hall on horseback, and fling down his glove, offering to do battle against anyone who should deny that the newly anointed sovereign was the lawful King of this realm. The office of King's champion has been held ever since the time of Richard II by the descendants of Sir John Dymoke, Lord of the Manor of Scrivelsby in Lincolnshire.

H.R.H. THE PRINCE OF WALES IN THE UNIFORM OF A COLONEL OF THE
WELSH GUARDS

Photo Press Portrait Bureau

H.R.H. THE PRINCESS ROYAL, THE KING'S ONLY DAUGHTER

Photo Press Portrait Bureau

HIS MAJESTY WITH THE DUKE OF YORK AND THE DUKE OF KENT

After the wedding of the King's niece, Princess Maud of Fife.

Photo Sport and General

One ancient and honourable office which has *not* fallen into disuse, however, is that of Earl Marshal, held as an hereditary post by the Dukes of Norfolk since the fifteenth century. As head of the College of Heralds, he has a great deal of hard work to do whenever a new reign begins, and even though it is no longer his duty to " appease all tumults and noise in the King's presence," or his privilege to receive as his fee " the horse and the palfrey on which the King and his Queen rode to their place of Coronation . . . and the chines of all swans and cranes served at the banquet," his responsibilities are many, and all the Royal commands connected with the ceremony in the Abbey are issued by him.

The Meaning of Kingship

And now that this many-coloured pageant has passed before our eyes, we may pause and ask ourselves, " What did it mean in the old days ? " and then, perhaps, " What does it all mean to-day ? "

Well, in the old days it meant that, by right of descent, and with the blessing of the Church and the sanction of traditional ceremony, one man had assumed tremendous powers over the lives of thousands of his fellow-men. A king was, in a sense, both a monarch and a priest. Before the Reformation " the anointed King was within his Realm the accredited Vicar of God for secular purposes " ; hence the priestly character of the vestments, linen robe, dalmatic, and stole, which he still wears at one stage in his coronation. Since the time of Henry VIII the English sovereign has also been the head of the Church of England. Anyone who knows anything about history will realize that right up to the beginning of the Georgian period, English kings could—in theory—do practically what they pleased. Some of them were clever enough to enlist the goodwill of their

' faithful Commons ' ; some were foolish enough to try to do without it ; but they all claimed to be answerable to God alone, and to be His direct representatives, " be the people never so impatient."

George I's ignorance of the English language and Sir Robert Walpole's ignorance of French led to the introduction of the Cabinet system of government ; and the gradual spread of modern theories, the slow, progressive widening of the franchise—which simply means, the granting of the right to vote to more and more people—have curtailed both the powers and the privileges of the sovereign.   What remains ?

Look at the " image and superscription " on a penny.   There you will see, set forth in fragments of Latin, that *Georgius V* is *Dei Gra. Britt. Omn. Rex Fid. Def. Ind. Imp.*—that is to say, that, by the Grace of God, he is King of all the Britains, Defender of the Faith, and Emperor of India.   Notice the first phrase—it is another link with the remote past.   We have not dropped the ancient idea that our kings reign ' by Divine Right,' although " the right divine of kings to govern wrong " *has* passed away. The next phrase is usually rendered, " of the British Dominions beyond the Sea," and a glance at any map where these dominions are marked in red will show you of what a vast realm George V is king.   The title of ' Defender of the Faith ' was given to Henry VIII by Pope Leo X as a reward for the Royal attack on Martin Luther, and has been rather quaintly retained by Henry's Protestant successors.   Disraeli made King George's grandmother, Queen Victoria, Empress of India in 1876, twenty years after the Government of India was taken over by the British Crown.

The English monarch no longer claims, as his ancestors did, to be King of France as well ; nor does he call himself Duke of Aquitaine, though he still rules as Duke of Normandy in the Channel Isles, where any of his lieges may invoke his protection in the formula used when the first Normans were lords of those Isles, " *Haro ! haro ! haro ! A l'aide, mon prince, on me fait tort !* " (" Help, my prince ! I am being wronged ! ") This cry was raised quite recently in the Channel Isles. His powers over the lives and fortunes of his subjects are no longer absolute, though in some ways they are greater than many of us realize. Nominally he reigns over a population of something like 483,370,000 men, women, and children, occupying an area of 13,909,782 square miles. The people are of every creed and colour, their homes are in every continent, washed by all the seas of the world. His Plantagenet ancestors held sway over a population of about five millions ! And their authority, which was believed to come direct from God Himself, extended over all these people, from the humble serf toiling in the fields to the great feudal baron who, at the king's command, had to lead his vassals to war. Those Plantagenet sovereigns, some of them excellent rulers, some of them very much the reverse, wielded spiritual as well as earthly powers. And among the marvellous gifts which a king was once supposed to possess by virtue of his kingship was the gift of healing, by the touch of his royal hand, the disease known as ' scrofula.' Edward III was the first English sovereign to ' touch for the King's Evil,' as the ailment used to be called ; the Tudors continued the ceremony—it was a solemn ceremony, accompanied by prayers and chants—and all the Stuarts carried out what must have been a decidedly painful duty for the benefit of their afflicted subjects. ' Touch-pieces,' specially struck gold medallions, were given to each sufferer to hang round his neck as a memento and a talisman in one. The Hanoverian dynasty, however, stoutly declined to conform to the ancient tradition !

Another historic ceremony in which the king no longer bears a personal part is the Royal Maundy, though, unlike ' touching for the King's Evil,' it has not been abolished altogether. On the Thursday next before Easter Sunday each king was wont, in commemoration of Christ's washing His Apostles' feet, to wash the feet of as many poor men as he was years of age. William III, a practical Dutchman, decided that his Court almoner should perform the duty in his stead, and in 1704, under George II, the actual foot-washing was abolished. But the almsgiving part of the ceremony was retained, and the Royal bounty is still bestowed every year, in the form of specially minted silver coins equal in number to the King's age, enclosed in silken purses, and distributed in Westminster Abbey by the Dean, as King's almoner.

Functions of the King To-day

Now, after this backward glance at some of the privileges and duties of King George's forerunners, let us return to the question, " What does it mean to be a King to-day ? " We do not have to know very much about it to see that it means heavy responsibility and hard work. It is impossible to look at an illustrated newspaper, or to watch a news-reel, without realizing that the King is a man of many interests and activities, who takes his royal duties very seriously and carries them out with unfailing energy. But what is his place in the modern state, which users of difficult words call ' the body politic ' ? Parliamentary government in the British Empire is founded on the ancient principle of hereditary kingship ; the crown is the keystone of the whole arch. But what can the King do ?

Well, in the first place it is rather startling to be told quite seriously that " the King can do no wrong." But, in a sense, it is true ; because he is above the law ! He could not be arrested, or put into prison, if he were to commit a crime. As for his public actions, the Parliamentary instruments to which he gives the Royal assent, those are the work of his Ministers, who, of course, *can* err—and not infrequently *do*. The nation holds that they are answerable for anything which the nation wishes to be altered, but the Crown remains aloof from the tumult of politics. And that is one of the best things about a constitutional monarchy like ours. *It goes on.* Parties rise and fall, slogans are shouted and forgotten, promises are made and broken, plans are laid down and may—or may not—be carried out. But the fact of Kingship continues, and supplies an element of steadiness in a changing world.

A constitutional monarchy combines the advantages of a Republic with those of a benevolent despotism. "The Crown," said a learned legal authority, " is the official representative of the community to carry out its wishes, as far as they are expressed or can be ascertained." But what, exactly, does the adjective ' constitutional ' mean in this country ? Nobody really knows, except that it is the reverse of ' unconstitutional.' The reason for this uncertainty is the vague and flexible character of the British Constitution. Unlike the Constitution of the United States of America, and of some of the smaller States created as the result of the Great War, ours has never been written down, so every one can interpret it in accordance with his own ideas, and nearly everybody is quite pleased with it. In a general way it is agreed that, though the Royal assent is necessary to every Bill, the King should not oppose the will of the people as manifested in Parliament ; and that he must not take any important step without the knowledge and approval of his Ministers. Yet he does still possess what is called ' the right of veto ' and could, if he wished, refuse to give the Royal assent to a Bill which he honestly believed to be contrary to the best interests of the nation. No king has actually done this since 1707, but the right to do it still exists. A more likely course would now be for the Sovereign to talk things over with his Ministers and, if they proved stubborn, to dissolve Parliament in the hope that a General Election would lead to the rejection of the obnoxious measure.

It is, as we shall see, in the King's name that Parliaments

are summoned and dissolved, ambassadors are sent to foreign powers, ports and harbours are appointed, judges and magistrates are chosen, and money is minted. Nor is the King's power merely nominal, though so often exercised through others. He could, if he liked, while Parliament is sitting, enter the House of Lords, seat himself upon the throne, desire the Commons to be summoned to the ' bar ' dividing the Upper from the Lower House, and there and then declare Parliament to be dissolved. He could make a declaration of war against any foreign power. He could dismiss the Privy Council and disband the Army. His personal privileges are many, and some of them are curious, such as the right to receive every sturgeon caught in British waters !

" The Sovereign has, under a constitutional monarchy such as ours, three rights—the right to be consulted, the right to encourage, the right to warn. A king of great sense and sagacity would want no others." Now that Queen Victoria's letters have been published we know how active she was in exercising all three rights, and already it has been made clear that King Edward's ministers gladly availed themselves of his naturally shrewd judgment and his remarkable personal knowledge of foreign affairs. As conversations between Cabinet Ministers and their Sovereign are ' strictly private and confidential,' and cannot be divulged without breaking a solemn oath, it is not possible for us to know to-day exactly when, or in what way, or to what extent, his present Majesty has influenced the course of history by being consulted, by giving encouragement, and by uttering words of warning. But we do know that he is kept in constant touch with everything that his Ministers are doing, or even thinking of doing, and that, by reason of his extensive travels within the British Empire and his practical interest in national affairs, he is excellently qualified to exercise the tradi-tional influence of the Throne.

A witty Englishman—it was Walter Bagehot—once said that " Royalty is a government in which the attention of the nation is concentrated on one person doing interesting actions ; a Republic is a government in which that attention is divided between many, who are all doing uninteresting actions." In the pages which follow you will learn something about some of those interesting actions, and you will see how in a modern world, full of scientific marvels and wonders of machinery, there is still a place, and a very great place, for an anointed king, ruling by the Grace of God.

BUCKINGHAM PALACE FROM ST JAMES'S PARK

Photo J. Dixon Scot

WINDSOR CASTLE FROM THE THAMES

Photo J. Dixon Scott

SANDRINGHAM

Photo J. Dixon Scott

BALMORAL CASTLE

Photo Valentine

II

KING, CHURCH, AND STATE

By

DOROTHY MARGARET STUART

KING, CHURCH, AND STATE

The King and the Church

YOU will remember that when the King was crowned the Archbishop of Canterbury used these words : " Be thy head anointed with holy oil, as kings, priests, and prophets were anointed " ; and also that, at one stage in the ceremony, he was arrayed in what may be called priestly vestments—a linen robe, a supertunica of cloth of gold, and an embroidered stole.

From the earliest times a king was looked upon as a sort of priest ; and in medieval days he was quaintly described as a *mixta persona*, a ' mixed person,' half-layman and half-ecclesiastic—something like Strephon, in Gilbert and Sullivan's opera, *Iolanthe*, who was half a mortal and half a fairy ! But it was not until Henry VIII broke away from the Church of Rome that the King of England claimed to be the actual head of the Church in England. It was because they denied this new and startling claim, as well as on account of their opposition to the divorce of Katharine of Aragon, that Thomas More and Bishop Fisher died the death of martyrs. At the present time the King is, in fact as well as in name, what Charles I called himself in 1628, "Supreme Governour of the Church within these Our Dominions."

The doctrine of the Church with regard to the State is stated in the twenty-seventh of the Thirty-Nine Articles of Religion, drawn up in the reign of Queen Elizabeth :

The Queen's Majesty hath the Chief Power in this Realm of England and other her Dominions, unto whom the chief Government of all

Estates of this Realm, whether they be Ecclesiastical or Civil, in all
causes doth appertain. . . .

When we attribute to the Queen's Majesty the chief Government
. . . we give not to our princes the ministering either of God's Word
or of the Sacraments . . . but that only prerogative which we see
to have been given always to all godly princes in holy Scriptures by
God Himself : that is, that they should rule all states and degrees
committed to their charge by God, whether they be Ecclesiastical or
Temporal, and restrain with the Civil Sword the stubborn and evil-
doers.

In the principal daily services of the Church of England this
threefold bond between Throne, Church, and State is expressed
in special prayers—prayers for the King and the Royal Family,
prayers for the High Court of Parliament, prayers beseeching
Divine aid " in times of War and Tumults," prayers of thanksgiving " for deliverance from our enemies," or for the restoration
of " Publick Peace at Home." In several of these the King is
described as " our King and Governour," an allusion to his
headship of the Church " as by law established," and in one
of them—the prayer for the High Court of Parliament, he is
called " our most religious and gracious King."

Church convocations are summoned and dissolved by the
Crown, and the Royal assent is necessary before the Church can
make any changes in ecclesiastical law. The great officers of
the Anglican Church are all appointed by the King, and of
these the Archbishops and certain of the Bishops sit in the
Houses of Lords under the title of Peers Spiritual. You will
remember them at the Coronation.

So little have things changed since Elizabethan days that a
famous lawyer of Queen Victoria's time wrote concerning her
what might have been written of Elizabeth herself, and what
might, altering the word ' Queen ' to ' King,' be written of
George V to-day : " The Queen is over all persons in all
causes, as well ecclesiastical as temporal, within her dominions
supreme."

PRINCESS ELIZABETH OF YORK

Photo Marcus Adams

PRINCESS MARGARET ROSE OF YORK

Photo Marcus Adams

LORD LASCELLES AND THE HONOURABLE GERALD LASCELLES, SONS OF THE
PRINCESS ROYAL

THE KING'S GRANDCHILDREN

Photo Graphic Photo Union

CHILDREN OF THE CHAPEL ROYAL
Photo Central Press

THE CORONATION DURBAR AT DELHI
Photo Central Press

gave up its hereditary revenues in exchange for a fixed income, called a ' Civil List.' At the accession of his granddaughter, Victoria, this Civil List was £385,000 a year : at the accession of his great grandson, Edward VII, it was raised to £470,000, and this is the sum at which it still stands. But it must be clearly understood that this did not mean that the National Exchequer was actually the poorer. The hereditary revenues surrendered by Queen Victoria amounted only to £245,000 a year : those surrendered by King Edward were £432,000. " The nation may therefore be said to have made a very advantageous bargain with the Crown," as Sir John Marriott observes, in his book on *English Political Institutions*. The difference between Queen Victoria's Civil List and the present King's Civil List is, as you can see, not so great as the difference between the sums surrendered by her and the sums surrendered by her son, the balance being in the favour of the nation.

His Majesty's Government

Now let us turn to the actual methods by which, under its ancient constitutional monarchy, this realm is governed. As everybody who takes any interest in the question is aware, we have a Two-Chamber system. That is to say, we have the House of Commons, an *elective* assembly, and the House of Lords, an *hereditary* assembly. Members of Parliament are chosen at General Elections by the votes of the people ; members of the Upper House sit there either because of their inherited rank, or because they have been, as the phrase goes, ' raised to the peerage.' The functions of the Upper House are largely to act as a brake upon the proceedings of the Lower House, to prevent impetuous or revolutionary legislation, to give an interval for second thoughts, and an opportunity for fuller and more dispassionate discussion. Even Republican countries like France and the United States of America recognize the value of such an institution and, though they have no House of Lords, they have a Second Chamber called a Senate.

Prime Minister and Cabinet

The Prime Minister, the link between the King and the Cabinet, and the Government of which he is the head receive their mandate from the people ; and every time the people change their mind, or decide that they want to see another political party in power, another Prime Minister ' kisses hands ' —another, but not necessarily one new to the job, because it has happened more than once that the turn of fortune's wheel has brought a statesman a second, or even a third time to the Prime Minister's official residence at 10 Downing Street, Whitehall. His Majesty's Government of to-day may be His Majesty's Opposition of to-morrow ; but whatever happens one of the ruling principles of our political system is that " *His Majesty's Government must be carried on.*"

What is the Cabinet ? In its present form it dates from the accession of the House of Hanover in 1714 ; but if it may be correctly described as a Committee of the Privy Council it goes back to Norman times, when there was a body of men known as the *Curia Regis.* Charles II, partly because he was intelligent and partly because he was indolent, objected to the slowness of his Privy Council's proceedings, and the exaggerated numbers composing it : he therefore split the Council up into small executive committees, in which we may see the germ of our modern Cabinet. It is certain that ever since Sir Robert Walpole took over the reins of government when George I came to the Throne, the Premier and the Cabinet Ministers of the day have been mainly responsible for the policy of the country.

Every Cabinet Minister must be a Privy Councillor as well, and is bound by the Privy Councillor's oath of secrecy. The Council now consists of nearly three hundred persons, including

THE OPENING OF THE MERSEY TUNNEL, 1934

Photo Central Press

THE GENTLEMAN-USHER OF THE BLACK ROD

By permission of the " Popular Encyclopædia "

NUMBER TEN DOWNING STREET

Photo J. Dixon Scott

all living Cabinet Ministers, past and present ; many of the chief officers of State ; the two Archbishops and the Bishop of London ; many of the peers who have held important admini- strative posts ; a number of judges, ex-judges, and statesmen belonging to the overseas Dominions ; and a sprinkling of dis- tinguished men of letters, physicians, ex-ambassadors, newspaper proprietors, and others. The powers of the Privy Council have dwindled in proportion as the authority of the Cabinet has grown : but it still has executive functions to perform, and meets frequently. Proclamations and Orders-in-Council are issued by the Sovereign ' in Council,' and it is ' in Council ' that Ministers take the oaths of office and kiss the King's hand, that newly- appointed bishops do homage, and that the High Sheriffs of the Counties are ' pricked.' (This last ceremony is a quaint one ; the names of the sheriffs-elect are written on a long scroll, and the Sovereign confirms the election by pricking the parchment with a golden bodkin opposite each name.)

Ordinary routine meetings of the Privy Council are not largely attended—three forms a quorum—but when the Council meets to proclaim the accession of a king the Councillors rally round in force. On such occasions the Lord Mayor of London has the traditional privilege of being present. Rather different in its functions is the Judicial Committee of the Privy Council, with four ' law lords ' at its head. This is a Committee of the Privy Council : its decisions must be unanimous : its judgments are embodied in Orders issued by the King ' in Council ' ; and it is, in fact, a Court of Appeal.

Although officially and legally there is no such a person as the Prime Minister—' First Lord of the Treasury ' is the correct term—the post he fills is one of great importance, and the right to select a suitable Minister is one of the most valuable pre- rogatives still remaining to the Crown. Of course, the King must choose from among the members of the party paramount in the

House, or, in a case of political crisis, when the government of the day is defeated in the House, but a general election is not thought desirable, from among the members of the next largest party. But choose he does ; and that is the meaning of the words used on such occasions, " The King sent for——" whomever he *did* send for. Although the Sovereign is never present at Cabinet meetings, he is kept in close touch with his Ministers, and it will readily be understood that the wheels of government would not run well if the First Lord of the Treasury, otherwise the Prime Minister, were not a person with whom the King found it possible to work in harmony.

That a constitutional English Sovereign may exercise a great and helpful influence upon the course of political history is made more and more clear as the secret history and the private documents of the Victorian period are revealed. Mr Gladstone wrote, " the acts, the wishes, the example of the Sovereign in this country are a real power. Parliaments and Ministers pass . . . but she is to them as the oak in the forest is to the annual harvest of the field." Those words were written in the days of our grandfathers and grandmothers—days which in some ways seem as remote as those of Queen Anne, but, in a changing world, they still represent an unchanging fact. Many of the outward symbols of royal authority are links with the far-off past, and some people think they are rusty old links which ought to be broken. It is a pity that anyone should fail to understand that such things are " the outward and visible sign " of one of the best elements in our national life.

The Royal Assent

Parliamentary procedure is rich in such survivals. For example, when a Bill has been passed by both Houses—the House of Commons and the House of Lords—it has to receive the Royal assent before it becomes an Act ; and that assent is

given in the ancient Norman-French formula, *Le Roy le veult*—
the King wills it. Even in the old days the King, when rejecting
a Bill, did not say *Le Roy ne le veult pas*—the King does *not* will it :
he said, more cautiously, *Le Roy s'avisera*—the King will think
about it—but everybody understood that the more he thought
about it, the less inclined would he be to give his Royal assent.

Another link with the past is the existence of the office of the
Gentleman Usher of the Black Rod, which is connected with the
Most Noble Order of the Garter. Black Rod, as the holder of
this office is usually called 'for short,' has to maintain order in
the House of Lords and to arrest peers for breaches of privilege.
On certain occasions it is his duty to summon the 'faithful commons' to the bar dividing their House from that of the Peers.
These occasions are the reading of the Speech from the Throne,
either by the King in person or by the Lord Chancellor on his
behalf, the opening or proroguing of Parliament, and the announcement that a Bill has received the Royal assent. When
Black Rod passes across that part of the floor which marks the
division between the two Houses, the doors of the Lower House
are always shut, and he has to knock three times with his ebony
wand before he is admitted and allowed to deliver his message.
His official costume is full Court dress, with ruffles, kneebreeches,
buckled shoes, and cocked hat, and he wears an elaborate gold
badge hanging from a chain round his neck.

The King's Speech is written actually by his Ministers for the
time being, and reflects the ideas and intentions of the political
party in office. When it is printed the possessive pronoun ' My '
is always given a capital ' M.'

The Opening of Parliament

Whenever a new Parliament has been elected the members,
having assembled in the House of Commons, are summoned by
Black Rod to hear the Lords Commissioners for the opening of

Parliament read their commission : the Commons then elect their Speaker, and on the following day they go with him to the House of Lords, to receive the royal approbation of their choice. This having been given—not, of course, by the King in person, but on his behalf—the Speaker lays claim, in the name of the Commons, to their " ancient and undoubted rights and privileges." Next, all the members take the oath " to be faithful and bear true allegiance to his Majesty," and in due course their old friend Black Rod visits them again and summons them to repair to the bar of the House of Lords to hear the King's Speech.

The King, accompanied by Queen Mary, has first driven in State from Buckingham Palace to Westminster, in a State Coach looking rather like the golden coach which Cinderella's godmother made by magic out of a pumpkin, escorted by Beefeaters on foot, and by Life Guardsmen on magnificent black horses. While the King is present in person in the Houses of Parliament the Royal Standard instead of the Union Jack is flown from the Victoria Tower.

The scene in the House of Lords is a picturesque one, especially on a grey winter morning, when the clusters of electric lights are dimmed until the arrival of the King and Queen. Peers in their robes of crimson and ermine fill the cross-benches and the seats ranged against the walls ; Lords of Appeal and Judges, all in their wigs of white horsehair, are grouped round the crimson Woolsack, the traditional seat of the Lord Chancellor of England since Elizabeth's reign. On each side of the cross-benches are triple rows of peeresses, their jewels flickering in the soft light. The lawn sleeves of the bishops make a splash of whiteness among all this crimson, and to the right of the still-empty throne sit foreign diplomats, many of them wearing uniforms of great splendour.

Everyone rises when a prince of the blood royal enters and, after bowing to the Throne, takes his place among the peers.

(The Prince of Wales sits alone, to the right of the Throne.) Then, suddenly, all the lamps go out, only to blaze forth in full glory a moment later as the King and Queen appear and walk slowly, hand in hand, to the dais from which the Speech is to be read. Each has two pages to carry the long, trailing royal robes which sweep behind them. The Sword of State is borne aloft by one peer, the Cap of Maintenance on a crimson cushion by another. The heralds in their many-coloured tabards gather beneath the steps of the dais. Beside the King's throne is the Queen's, and behind the Queen's throne her ladies-in-waiting stand. " My Lords," says the King in a clear voice, " pray be seated." There is a rustle of robes as the peers obey.

Black Rod now departs to summon the " faithful Commons," and soon the Prime Minister, the Speaker, and their colleagues make their appearance, the other M.P.'s huddling in a tight jam behind them. It is now time for the King to read his Speech, which he does standing. Those of us who have heard him broadcast know what a deep and distinct voice he has, and how well every syllable he utters can be heard. Unless in times of wars and tumults, the speech from the Throne usually begins with these words, which one is sure that the King must be glad to repeat : " My relations with foreign Powers continue to be friendly," and it always ends with this pious aspiration, " And I pray that the blessing of Almighty God may rest upon your deliberations."

At the conclusion of this ceremony the King and Queen rise, bow to the company, which has risen with them, and bows low in response. They then depart with the same dignity as they came.

Taxes and Customs

Those of us who are neither too young nor too poor to pay Income Tax are only too well aware that the communications sent to us by the tax-collectors arrive in long buff envelopes marked " On His Majesty's Service." Although it is the Chancellor of the Exchequer for the time being who decides the amount we must pay, and though it is the Commissioners of Inland Revenue who receive our payments, the necessary legislation needs the Royal assent, and Finance Bills, like all other Bills, are described as having been made " by the King's most excellent Majesty by and with the advice of the Lords, spiritual and temporal, and Commons in this present Parliament assembled, and by the authority of the same." The taxes themselves are often called ' the King's Taxes,' just as the dues payable on certain imported goods at custom-houses are called ' the King's Customs.' It is because such custom-houses are necessarily situated at seaport towns that one of the royal prerogatives is concerned with appointing what seaports shall and what shall not be regarded as ' harbours ' from the point of view of the Customs.

Another department of the State with which the Crown is associated, though less closely than in bygone years, is the administration of justice. When anybody brawls or creates a disturbance he is said to ' break the King's Peace ' ; judges, magistrates, and all those who have authority to administer the law and to punish wrongdoers, are appointed by the Crown, in accordance with advice tendered by its councillors. In theory, if not in everyday practice, the King is the Chief Magistrate of England, the final judge by whom all causes could be decided and all other decisions set aside. Actually, of course, judicial functions are performed by officers of the law on behalf of the Crown, interpreting the promise made so reluctantly by King John at Runnymede, " To none will we sell, to none will we deny or delay, right or justice."

The King's Bench

The very name of the Supreme Court of Justice tells us something of its history, for it is called the King's Bench. In early days the 'bench' was the seat upon which the monarch sat to administer justice in person. The Lord Chancellor and the Lord Chief Justice, as well as the Law Officers of the Crown, the Solicitor-General and the Attorney-General, are the instruments of royal equity. Barristers who have attained a certain degree of distinction in their profession are made K.C.'s, or 'King's Counsel learned in the law,' and are said to have 'taken silk,' as their gowns are then made of silken instead of woollen stuff. These gentlemen are not actually expected to give the King the benefit of their personal advice, but the title they bear is evidence of the connexion between Crown, Bench, and Bar.

Even when a King of England or of France himself sat as judge to hear the complaints of his subjects and to see that right was done, there had to be men working as his agents and interpreters, or the whole primitive system of law and justice would have broken down. Kings have always been compelled to delegate some of their powers and duties to others, and at the present time a bewildering number of officials have the honourable responsibility of acting on behalf of the King. Such are his ambassadors, always described in official documents as the Ambassadors of His Britannic Majesty ; these are his diplomatic messengers to foreign countries, and the Embassies where they reside are British territory, no matter in what part of the world or in whose dominions they may be.

"By tradition," says Sir John Marriott, "the King has always played a more direct part in Foreign than in Home affairs." Foreign ambassadors in England are 'accredited' to the King personally, though when they take up their duties they are presented at the Court of St James's by the Foreign Secretary of the day. All dispatches of any importance addressed to the Governments of other countries are read by the King and receive his assent.

The King's Messengers

Confidential documents, often in cipher, are not entrusted to the ordinary post office, although the mails carried by the G.P.O. are the King's Mails. To a special body of cool, experienced, and resourceful men, known as the King's Messengers, is given the important and sometimes perilous duty of carrying such documents from one country to another. The passports of these Messengers are easily recognized, for they are red in colour : their distinctive badge is a silver medallion bearing the royal monogram encircled by the Garter motto, and tipped with a small silver model of a greyhound.

The Post Office is a Government department : but, as we shall see, it is the direct descendant of the Royal Post of the sixteenth century, and it retains its kingly associations, as you know, from the royal monogram and crown on the pillar-boxes and on the gaily-painted mail-vans.

In the old days great Kings would appoint powerful vassals to rule over conquered provinces or distant dukedoms on their behalf : in the same way King George delegates his kingly functions to Viceroys and Governors-General, who receive the same salutes, honours, and tributes that would be offered to him if he were present in person.

Every day we see many things which, if we pause to think about them a little, will remind us of the King. We have just mentioned the pillar-boxes and the mail-vans. The King's portrait, often with the Queen, sometimes with their children or grandchildren, is familiar to us all. We see it on the ' movie '-screen, in the newspapers, in the shop-windows, on the walls of houses, and on postage stamps and coins.

AT SUNDERLAND IN 1918
A very youthful breadwinner.
Photo Central Press

THE KING ON CLYDESIDE
A chat with a Scottish workman.
Photo Sport and General

QUEEN MARY BEATING TIME TO COMMUNITY SINGING

Photo Graphic Photo Union

AT A BOY SCOUTS' RALLY: THE KING IS AMUSED

Star Photo

The Royal Mint

The Royal Mint is a much more ancient royal concern than the Royal Mail, and goes back to the time of Canute, whose rebuking of his flattering courtiers on the seashore is almost as well known as Alfred's burning of those unlucky cakes. At one time each of the large provincial towns had its own mint, and struck its own coins, though all such coins had to bear the head of the reigning Sovereign. Mints still work separately in Australia, Canada, India, and the Union of South Africa, and in all those outposts of the Empire the profile of the King-Emperor is within the ken of every child.

Nor is it only through our eyes that we are reminded of the King whose Silver Jubilee we are celebrating. There is one tune we all recognize whenever we hear the first notes played or sung—a solemn and yet vigorous tune, simple and easy both to remember and to sing—a tune we shall all hear often in 1935 —for it is our National Anthem, *God Save the King*.

THE KING, WITH THE DUKE OF YORK AND THE CHIEF SCOUT, INSPECTING BOY SCOUTS

"Daily Mirror" Photograph

THE KING TALKING TO A SMALL PATIENT AT THE PRINCESS LOUISE HOSPITAL
FOR CHILDREN

Photo Sport and General

SHADWELL SCHOOL CHILDREN CHEERING THE KING AND QUEEN

Photo Central Press

III

IN THE KING'S SERVICE

ALL loyal subjects are 'in the King's service,' for if his Majesty called upon them to do their part to help in any emergency they would gladly hasten to serve him as best they could, from the Boy Scout who, by earning his cyclist badge, pledges himself to ride on duty if the need arises, to the veteran who in the time of national crisis offers his services in whatever capacity he may.

Although we cannot in our everyday life do much more than rise to our feet when the National Anthem is played and raise our hats when the King passes by, it is interesting to learn something about the people who give his Majesty personal service, and about those who, wearing his uniform, have under-taken to defend the Empire of which he is the head.

The Royal Household

Every Court has attached to it a large number of officials of varying ranks. Most of them hold offices that have come down through the centuries, and some have the most curious titles.

First comes the Lord Steward whose duties have very largely lapsed, but who appears on ceremonial occasions, when he carries a white staff in the Royal presence.

It is the Lord Chamberlain who has the most responsible post of all in the Household, for he is in charge of all Court ceremonial, and has to oversee the furnishing of the various palaces and the care of the pictures and works of art that are housed in them. At his office an immense amount of work goes

4

on, which involves a large staff of secretaries and clerks to cope with all the business that is daily transacted there. For instance, the Lord Chamberlain issues, at the King's command, the invitations for all Court functions, including Court presentations, the Royal Garden Parties, and the Royal Enclosure at Ascot. He also is responsible for the arrangements for royal weddings or funerals, for royal visits or visitors.

One of the Lord Chamberlain's staff is called the Reader or Examiner of Plays. You must have noticed on London theatre-programmes that it is always stated that the Lord Chamberlain has approved the play ; this is because he has power to refuse to license it to be performed, if he thinks fit. The Master of the Revels used to read and approve the plays in just the same way in the days of Queen Elizabeth. You will also notice that he has to satisfy himself that managers of theatres take proper precautions in case of fire, and have safety curtains and enough exits and wide passages, and this information, too, is printed on the programme.

The Master of the Horse is the third officer of importance. He has charge of everything to do with the Royal Mews and marshals the carriages or cars in the royal processions.

Have you ever wondered why a stable is so often called a mews ? Originally the Royal Mews meant the place where the King's falcons were kept or ' mewed '—gradually the word came to mean an enclosure, and so a place for keeping or enclosing horses.

Twenty years ago there were a hundred and forty horses in the Royal Stables, now there are seventy—fifty-four carriage- and sixteen riding-horses. Anzac, the King's old charger, is ending his days peacefully at Hampton Court, and the King now rides Brownie, a bay horse, on parade, but uses a chestnut, Arabian Night, for hacking in the Park.

No longer do the famous eight creams draw the State Coach

in which the King and Queen drive to the Opening of Parliament ; their place has been taken by eight bays, which can be seen at home standing in their airy well-lit stalls, each with a green plate overhead, on which his name is lettered in gold. The horses used for the State Coach are easily distinguished as they seem to tower over the smaller carriage pairs and saddle-horses. The only lady of the party is the mare Laurestinus, who has Butterfly for her stable companion. Then there are Blake and Van Tromp, two bright bays ; Highlander and Roysterer, Cadogan and Rodney, Ploughboy and Red Knight, and many more. Among the riding-horses is Markree, an Irish mare, with Cæsar and Viking as her companions.

The timing of the royal processions is always judged to the minute. Four grey horses draw the King's semi-state road landau, and they trot one mile in eight minutes. The walking speed of a procession is about three and a half miles an hour, and, of course, when the State Coach is used it goes at walking pace, with the Beefeaters escorting it on either side.

The eleven royal cars and lorries also come under the orders of the Master of the Horse. The cars used by the King and Queen are painted maroon, picked out with red, with the Royal Crown on the doors, and on special occasions a large red crown is fixed in front to the roof of the car. The King always has a second car in attendance when he goes by road, but the Queen does not, and once or twice she has accepted the services of a private car offered to her when her own broke down. Imagine the chance of being able to drive the Queen back to the Palace in your own car ! It is said that when this happened actually in London, the gate-keeper at the special Palace entrance was so surprised at seeing an ordinary car drive up for admittance that there was quite a long delay before he realized that the Queen was really inside. A new twelve-cylinder Double-Six Daimler was ordered as the State car a few months ago.

Only the King may go through the great gates of the Wellington Arch at the top of Constitution Hill, and through Admiralty Arch at the end of the Mall, but when paying private visits, his chauffeur obeys traffic lights and police signals just like an ordinary driver, for the King is always particularly anxious not to inconvenience the public more than is necessary. He constantly thinks of them in details such as ordering his car windows to be extra large, so that people can have a really good view of himself and the Queen when passing, which they all love to do, and he will not allow them to be turned off the steps of the Queen Victoria Memorial in front of Buckingham Palace if they want to see better from there.

We seem to have come a long way from the Master of the Horse, but he is very much concerned with all these affairs.

The office of Gold-Stick-in-Waiting is very ancient; Silver Stick acts as his deputy when he is away.

In 1528 there was a plot against the life of King Henry VIII, and it was ordered that a commander in the Household Cavalry should always attend the King with a gold-headed ebony staff, and a second officer of lower rank would occasionally relieve him, carrying a silver-headed ebony staff. They were to be responsible for the personal safety of the King whenever he waked, from the moment he rose in the morning to the time he went to bed, except in the royal bedchamber.

To-day the Gold Stick and Silver Stick are two officials who represent the Household Brigade at Court—that is to say, the cavalry escort as opposed to the foot guards.

The youngest members of the Household are the Pages of Honour, whose appointment is in the gift of the King, and who are usually the sons of members of the Royal suite, or of personal friends of the King. They serve as Pages from the age of eleven and must resign at sixteen and a half; they are summoned

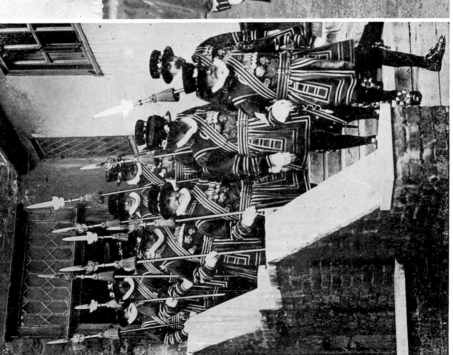

THE YEOMEN OF THE GUARD AT WESTMINSTER ABBEY ON A
MAUNDY THURSDAY

Photo Graphic Photo Union

THE KING REVIEWING THE ARCHERS OF HIS SCOTTISH BODYGUARD

Photo Central Press

"KING GEORGE'S KEYS"

The nightly ceremony at the Tower of London

Photo Sport and General

PLANTING A TREE AT THE ROYAL AGRICULTURAL COLLEGE, CIRENCESTER

Photo Sport and General

to attend all State ceremonies as train-bearers to their Majesties.

At Court functions the Pages stand behind the Throne. If they are summoned in the holidays they have to give up anything they have planned to do in order to obey the King's command, and in term time they may have to miss a day at school if Court duty calls them.

Other important members of the Household are the King's Private Secretary, who is his own personal secretary and works closely with him every day, the Keeper of the Archives, and the Vice-Chamberlain. But many of the quaint old titles and offices have long ago died out, and there is now no Rat-Killer to his Majesty, with his salary of £100 a year, and no " Master of the Game of Boarrs and Bulls," or of the Game of Cock-fighting. The Keeper of the Swans still remains, and also his Majesty's Bargemaster, who steers the royal barge of over 240 years old, when it is rowed (very rarely) by eight royal bargemen on the Thames.

The Yeomen of the Guard

When you think of how the King is guarded in his Palace or when he travels about, you probably think first of the sentries marching up and down outside the gates, or of the police lining the streets as he passes, or of the naval escort when he puts to sea. But you must not forget that the oldest Royal Bodyguard in England is now stationed at the Tower of London, and at once you will guess that these are the famous Beefeaters or Yeomen of the Guard. King Henry VII founded them " for the security of his person," and incorporated with them the ancient body of the Yeomen Warders of the Tower.

In those days the Guard was a band of fifty archers, some called Tent Pitchers, others called Yeomen Rangers, who looked after the tapestries in the royal palaces.　There were two others known as Yeomen Bedgoers, and they were in charge of his Majesty's beds when travelling, and saw that no enemy of the King lay hidden under the coverings and hangings.

It was the Yeomen of the Guard who discovered and seized Guy Fawkes when he was hiding in the vaults of the Houses of Parliament at the time of the Gunpowder Plot, and to this day it is their duty to march through these vaults with halberds and lanterns at the opening of each new session.

The last time an English king led his troops in actual warfare was when George II took part in the battle of Dettingen, and after that the Yeomen's privilege of attending the Sovereign on the field of battle lapsed.　But they still march in procession as a bodyguard on both sides of the State Coach in their royal red tunics, embroidered with Tudor Roses, kneebreeches, scarlet stockings, and the well-known flat hat and white ruff.

There are various opinions as to why the Yeomen were called Beefeaters ; one theory is that the name goes back to 1669, when the Grand Duke of Tuscany was so impressed by the magnificent King's Guard, that he wrote : " They are great eaters of beef, of which a very large ration is given them daily at the Court, and they might be called Beefeaters ! "

But by far the most attractive story is the one related by Fuller, which is worth telling in full.

> Once, while on a hunting expedition at Reading Abbey, Henry VIII dressed himself in the uniform of one of his Yeomen of the Guard, and having so disguised himself, paid a visit to the Abbot about dinner-time.
>
> Being apparently one of the King's retinue, he received welcome from the Abbot, and was invited to dine at his own table.　The principal dish was a large joint of beef, and the King being " hungry as a hunter " ate heartily, yea, voraciously of the meat.
>
> The Abbot, observing his evident enjoyment, addressed him, saying, " Well fare thy heart !　And here in a cup of sack I remember the health of his Grace, your master.　I would an hundred pounds

if I could eat as heartily of beef as you. Alas, my weak and squeamish stomach will hardly digest a piece of a small rabbit or a chicken."

After courteous thanks the guest departed.

In a few weeks after, the Abbot was committed, he knew not why, a close prisoner to the Tower, and his food was limited to the usual prison fare—bread and water—and with this he had to be content for some time. At last to his surprise and delight, a joint of beef was put before the prisoner, and he attacked it with gusto. While so employed, the Abbot was astonished to see the King enter the room, and demand a hundred pounds of him for having restored to him his lost appetite for roast beef.

The money was ultimately paid and the prisoner released, and ever thereafter, whenever the Abbot saw a Yeoman of the Guard, he thought of the " beef-eater," and the King in disguise as a Yeoman of the Guard.

We cannot leave the Yeomen at the Tower in their picturesque uniform, without remembering the ancient ceremony of the King's Keys, nightly performed within the building. For centuries it has taken place, and the Keys of five reigning Georges, of the two Charles's, and of Elizabeth have been carried and saluted.

When Queen Victoria died on a January night in the early evening, the new King, Albert Edward, had to decide by which name he would be known, and this could not be announced immediately. But at the Tower the ceremony of the Keys had to go forward as usual, until there came the answer to the challenge, when the name of the Sovereign must always be given. For sixty-three years the word ' King ' had not been heard at the Tower, but that night the reply was hesitatingly given of " The King's Keys." The next night the correct formula was used, and the answer made—" King Edward's Keys."

Latterly this lovely old ceremony has been broadcast from the Tower in the summer, and we have been able actually to hear the tread of the escort and the martial ring of their arms. When the time approaches, the escort is met by the Chief Warder, carrying the bunch of keys in his hand. As they pass, sentries present arms, and the Warder proceeds to the Main Gate, and there asks for 'the escort for the Keys.' A sergeant and four privates are detailed to act as escort, and one carries the lantern to light the way as the little procession goes from gate to gate.

The Barrier Gate, the Middle Tower, and lastly the Byward Tower are locked in turn, and the escort presents arms at each; then the Keys are marched to the Main Guard, but immediately they go under the dark arch of the Bloody Tower, leading to the Inner Ward, a sentry challenges :

" Halt ! Who comes there ? "

The Chief Warder answers :

" The Keys."

" Whose keys ? " comes the challenge again.

" King George's Keys."

" Advance, King George's Keys. All's well." The escort proceeds on its way until it reaches the Main Guard, which has already turned out under the command of an officer.

" Guard and escort, present arms," comes the order, and it is then that the Chief Warder steps forward and, taking off his hat, cries : " God preserve King George ! " and a loud " Amen " is given in answer.

The Keys are deposited in the King's House for delivery to the Governor, and there they remain for the night in safe keeping.

The Honourable Corps of Gentlemen-at-Arms

Not content with the ' band of fifty archers ' instituted by his father as his special bodyguard, Henry VIII determined to have a grander guard, which was to " exceed in magnificence and expense any contemplated by his predecessors."

The easiest way to make it grander was to recruit it from men who owned land and horses, and who could therefore give more in the way of service than others who had not such possessions to dispose of.

So King Henry created another ' immediate Guard of the

Sovereign,' whom he called his Pensioners or Spears, and they, in addition to pledging themselves to defend him against all foes, also promised each to keep three horses and two servants for the royal service, and this promise has never been withdrawn down to the present day, though several of the present Honourable Corps might be hard put to it to produce the horses on demand !

They carry small battle-axes covered with crimson velvet on State occasions to-day, but within living memory were prepared to fight in defence of St James's Palace, when there were fears of a Chartist outbreak in London. Nowadays you may see in the paper the announcement that " his Majesty's Bodyguard of the Honourable Corps of Gentlemen-at-Arms were on duty in the Throne Room at an Investiture, under the command of the Captain, and that the Lieutenant, the Clerk of the Cheque, and the Harbinger were also on duty." These are the same old titles of the officers just as they were in King Henry VIII's time, and they are very proud of them.

The Royal Company of Archers

When King James I of England (and VI of Scotland) was on the Throne, he was tremendously keen on archery, and most anxious that it should not die out as a sport. He even went so far as to issue an order, which said that the King decreed " that na man play at the fute-ball, under the paine of fiftie schillings," lest archery practice should be interfered with. It seems a long way from the quiet skill of the archery ground to the seething excitement of a Cup Tie final !

It is said that King James formed, like his predecessors, a bodyguard of archers, and over the water there were also the famous Scottish Archer-Guard of France, the most faithful servants that the French king possessed. He kept twenty-four of them for his especial protection.

Years afterwards, towards the end of the century, when the Archers had gradually diminished, the Company was revived in Scotland, and firmly established, with a right to practise archery within the city walls of Edinburgh. They wore no special uniform then, but had " the Company's Seal and Arms on their Hatts or Bonnetts," and then Queen Anne gave the Royal Company its charter on which it is still constituted.

So we find the Scottish Archers on duty as Queen Victoria's Scottish Bodyguard at the great review of the Volunteers of Scotland, when the rain poured in torrents, and the Archers, some of them well on in years, stood proudly and uncomplaining for long hours on duty, their uniforms soaked and ruined.

Again in 1911 they were inspected by King George, who presented them with new Colours to replace those last given to them by William IV.

The King said : " I am very glad to have had this opportunity of inspecting the Royal Company of Archers, my Bodyguard in Scotland, and I congratulate you upon to-day's strong muster. I shall always watch over the welfare of the Royal Archers with that interest and solicitude shown by my predecessors."

To be a member of the Royal Company is indeed a privilege of which to be proud.

The Royal Navy

Alfred the Great is often called the founder of the British Navy. He was certainly the first King of England to realize that the only way to defeat an invader was to go forth and meet him on the sea, instead of waiting till he had gained a foothold on the land. Alfred's fleet probably consisted of three hundred swift ships, driven by oars as well as by sails.

When, one hundred and sixty-five years after Alfred's death, William the Norman sailed for England, the English Navy had dwindled almost to nothing, and not a single English ship put out to meet him as he approached the Sussex coast. With "seven hundred ships save four" he invaded the island which he claimed as his, and where he established the dynasty whence comes our reigning Royal House.

William's descendant, Richard Cœur de Lion, took a practical interest in ships, which he needed as transports when he embarked for Cyprus on his way to take part in the Third Crusade. His 'fleet' of two hundred gaily painted vessels was led by his favourite ship, *Trenc-la-mer*, or 'Cleave the Sea,' which carried a mighty lantern at the poop to guide the rest after dusk had fallen. Henry V was, however, the first king to appreciate the importance of the Navy from the point of view of commerce as well as the national defence, and if he had not been cut off in his early prime he would have raised England to the position of a first-class naval Power.

Henry VII, despite the proverbial Tudor caution in the matter of money, did a great deal for the Navy. To the Naval Comptroller of his son, Henry VIII, belongs the credit of setting up a body—Trinity House—which should license pilots and maintain beacons, buoys, and lighthouses. To the second Tudor was due the innovation of paying salaries to admirals, captains, and seamen, but the Navy was still regarded as a sort of seagoing branch of the fighting forces of the country. Each ship was manned by hired soldiers, with a small crew of seamen to navigate her. All the Tudors were conscious of the importance of sea-power, though it was not until the reign of the last and greatest of them that England's might was demonstrated on the sea.

And so through the years the Navy became more and more the safeguard and pride of all Englishmen, until as the Senior Service to-day, the men serving in his Majesty's ships are protecting his Dominions all over the world, for, as the old Naval Act runs, on the Navy, "under the good Providence of God, the

wealth, safety, and strength of the Kingdom chiefly depend."
In this very year of grace, General Hertzog, Premier of the Union
of South Africa, speaking at Cape Town, said, " The British Navy
means exactly the same to me as to an Englishman, because the
freedom of my people and my country are just as dependent on
it as England herself."

The King, who is always regarded as the Head of the Navy,
served in it for a considerable time as a young man, and only
left it because of the sudden death of his elder brother, the Duke
of Clarence, which made him the direct heir to the Throne.

He was promoted Admiral in 1907, and Admiral of the Fleet
in 1910, which rank he now holds. He is greatly concerned
with all that happens to the Fleet, and one of his first acts after
his Coronation was to spend a week at Portsmouth going thor-
oughly into the new schemes then under discussion. He was
always interested in submarines and insisted on submerging
in one of the earliest types.

The Navy is a sure shield of defence to this country, even
to-day when we are also looking for protection in the air. It
must never be forgotten that it is on the Navy in time of war
that we rely to guard our merchant vessels which bring food to
these shores, and that without it England would very soon have
a starving population. The courage and unadvertised heroism
of the men in the Fleet, from submarines to the greatest Dread-
nought, are things of which we cannot ever be proud enough ;
these men do not speak for themselves, little is written of them ;
and it is right that we should realize the hazards to which they
are exposed, and what our Navy is to us.

The Army

The British Army can trace its history back to the time when
the early Britons, armed with javelins and rude weapons of
various kinds, rushed into the sea to drive off Julius Cæsar and

THE KING CLIMBING UP FROM A SUBMARINE DURING A ROYAL INSPECTION OF THE GRAND FLEET

Photo Central Press

THE ROYAL YACHT *VICTORIA AND ALBERT*

Photo Sport and General

THE KING AND QUEEN TALKING TO " BERTIE," THE MASCOT
OF THE ROYAL SCOTS

Photo Sport and General

WITH THE CHILDREN OF THE MEN OF THE TANK CORPS AT TIDWORTH

Photo Central Press

his invading Romans, but the date of the birth of the Regular
Standing Army is considered to be 1660, the date of the Restoration of Charles II.

The relations of the King and the Army are very close, for
every soldier takes an oath of allegiance to King George V, his
heirs and successors, and every officer receives his commission
in the King's name.

It has been said that " at home, the forces of the Crown are
set not only for the protection of the King's Throne, but for the
maintenance of the King's peace." That is well said and very
true.

Many who cannot remember the anxious days of war must
feel a thrill when they read and are told of the gallantry of the
King's forces in the field, the hardships they bore, their amazing
endurance and stubborn resistance in the face of overwhelming
odds.

Since the War the Army has changed considerably, and no
one has been more interested than the King in the new schemes.

To-day, instead of holding ceremonial reviews and parades,
the King will often be found making a personal visit to army
workshops, sports-grounds, cook-houses, and to the army schools.
He will seldom miss the final of the Army Soccer Cup, and it is
that sporting element running right through British Army life
that makes it so different from some of the more military-minded
organizations of other countries.

" How long does it take to clean your white sheepskin ? "
asked Queen Victoria of an astonished trooper of the Life
Guards.

" Thirty hours, your Majesty," he managed to say.

" That is too much work. The Life Guards, I think, should
have *black* sheepskins," said the Queen, and black sheepskins over
the saddles of one regiment were a familiar sight until recent years.

The King is a Field Marshal in the Army. Though we are

not—and never were—a military nation, we have a wonderful tradition of valour in the field to uphold, and our King must be a soldier.

The Royal Air Force

The King is the Chief of the Royal Air Force, the first English King to bear the title. It seems very strange to us, who now take flying as an everyday occurrence, and hardly look up when an aeroplane drones overhead, that the original Royal Flying Corps was formed by Royal Warrant so short a time ago as 1912, though there had been a Balloon School at Chatham over thirty years before.

The first 'plane to take part in the Great War landed in France on August 13, 1914, and there were only 150 machines ready for service, and less than 250 pilots to fly them. They existed solely to supply the Army with extra eyes, acting as its long-distance telescopes. We can hardly believe that the German Higher Command did not know at the time that our Expeditionary Force had crossed the Channel since no Air Scouts were there to tell them.

Our squadrons had no distinguishing marks in the early days of the War. It was impossible to tell them from enemy machines at any height, so a Union Jack in the form of a shield was painted on the under side of the lower planes of British aircraft in the hope that that would solve the difficulty. But it was soon found that only the red crosses showed when they were high up, and that confused them with the black crosses of the enemy, so there had to be a change, and this time three red, white, and blue rings were painted, which have been used for our Air Force machines ever since.

Until 1918 the Royal Flying Corps was scouting and bombing for the Army, and the Royal Naval Air Service was protecting the ships and our eastern coasts, but in that year the two were amalgamated to form the Royal Air Force, so that each branch should keep in closer touch with the other, and both then came under the newly formed Air Council as one Service.

The heroism of the men on both sides who flew and fought in the War is a story that cannot be told here, but it can never be forgotten. The King calls the R.A.F. " the third arm of the defences of the Empire," and in his service both men and officers have already created a wonderful tradition in this the youngest branch of his Majesty's Services.

Two Orders of Knighthood

The most celebrated Order of Knighthood which the King can confer on his subjects or on any foreign personage whom he wishes to honour is the Garter, first instituted by Edward III.

Everyone knows the motto of the Garter, *Honi soit qui mal y pense*—but the origin of it is never quite decided. Some say that Edward III picked up the garter of Lady Salisbury at a Court ball, and seeing some of the courtiers tittering, made the famous remark, and others that it was the Queen's garter that gave rise to it on a similar occasion. Another theory is that Edward used his garter as a signal for battle at Crécy, and initiated the Order in memory of the day, but if this is so, why the motto ?

Whatever the origin, it is the most famous British Order, to which only twenty-five Knight Companions are admitted besides the King himself, the Queen, the Prince of Wales, and certain other Sovereigns.

The robes of the Order are quite magnificent. The mantle is of purple velvet lined with white taffeta, having the badge of the Order on the left shoulder ; the surcoat is of crimson velvet ; the hat is of black velvet, crowned with a mass of white ostrich and dark-coloured heron plumes. The Garter itself, of blue embroidered with gold, is worn under the left knee. From the golden collar hangs an enamelled figure of St George slaying the Dragon.

Black Rod, whom we have already met, is one of the officers of the Order, who carries a black rod " to apprehend delinquents and such as have offended against the Statutes." He has to attend at the Feast of St George, and at all other functions of the Order.

King Henry IV is said to have instituted the Order of the Bath on the day of his Coronation, but many people think that it goes back hundreds of years before that, to the days when warriors rode about the countryside rescuing damsels in distress, fighting for honour and glory (and sometimes for ransom money), but always out to do brave deeds and to place their services at the disposal of the King if need arose.

Those were the times when men wore armour, and the story goes that on one occasion when a doughty fighter was brought to the King for knighthood, he sent him away to be given " fresh raiment, sustenance, and a bath," so much was he in need of honest soap and water !

Actually the bath came to be looked upon as the spiritual purification of the knight before he took the oath of chivalry. But it seems clear, at any rate, from the writings of the old chroniclers, that the original ceremonies of initiation were most quaint, and no less than forty-six knights-to-be were conducted at the Tower of London through much elaborate ritual before King Henry's coronation.

In the White Tower were placed forty-six baths filled with warm water, draped with linen sheets, into which the knights stepped. Then with all pomp and majesty the King entered, and dipping his finger in the water " made the sign of the Cross on each bare back."

Eventually the knights rested in the beds which were provided behind each bath, before kneeling in the Chapel of St John all night in vigil beside their arms.

THE KING AND QUEEN, ATTENDED BY THEIR PAGES, IN A PROCESSION OF
KNIGHTS OF THE GARTER AT WINDSOR

St George's Chapel in the background.

Photo Central Press

CHRISTMAS MAILS READY TO BE TAKEN ABOARD THE *EMPRESS OF BRITAIN*

Fox Photos

AIR MAILS BEING LOADED AT CROYDON

Fox Photos

Nowadays the Knight-elect comes before the King and bows three times as he advances. He kneels on the right knee, and the King places the Order round his neck, and taking a sword strikes him on both shoulders, saying, " Rise, Sir ——" mentioning the Christian name of the knight. The latter rises, kisses the King's hand, and bows himself backward out of the room.

There are now three classes of the Order : Knights Grand Crosses, Knights Commanders, and Companions of the Order.

The Royal Mail

Every postman who knocks loudly at your door is on the King's service, for he is the bearer of the Royal Mail, though we take him so much for granted that this would seldom occur to us. The hurrying red mail-vans, the red pillar-boxes which delight foreigners, and on which are the royal monograms, the blue ones for Air Mails, the flag flown by mail steamers to show the precious freight they are carrying, even the King's head on our stamps—all these things are so familiar to us that we never give a thought as to how they ' happened,' or whether they have always been the same.

Different indeed they were. The delivery of letters or despatches goes back to very ancient times, when rulers wanted to keep in touch with their outlying governors. King Cyrus, who lived hundreds of years before Christ, had a regular courier service, and the Romans had amazingly swift means of communication by runners when they occupied Britain. The mail service was used mainly for sending State papers, but it was also used as a secret-service agency even in the days of Oliver Cromwell.

Queen Elizabeth was the first to try to establish a monopoly of the post, but only in so far as it affected foreign letters ; a few years later James I extended it to all letters in Great Britain, and the charges for using it went to the State. Everything had to

5

be sent to London first to be sorted, and as letters were not only charged by weight but by distance as well, it was extremely expensive.

After the days of runners, came those of post-boys, who rode across country with their post-bags, liable to be attacked by robbers, and altogether rather unreliable 'postmen.' Then there was an effort made to have special mail-coaches, as carts were so slow, and people were beginning to make a habit of wrapping up letters as parcels and sending them in the care of the coach-guard, who might or might not deliver them at their nearest destination.

The mail-coach from London to Holyhead took twenty-seven hours, and forty-three to Edinburgh, but such were the coach-robberies on the King's Highway that each mail-guard carried a blunderbuss, pistols, and a cutlass to protect his passengers and his mails. Then came the railways, and the decline of the good old coaching days ; after that the motor-van, and now the mail-carrying aeroplane, so that only in the far-away corners of the King's Dominions are his mails delivered by runner or horseman in historic fashion.

IV
THE KING AND HIS PEOPLE

By

M. C. CAREY

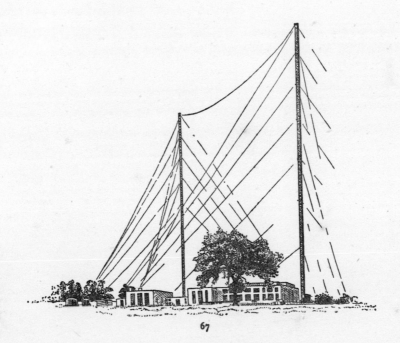

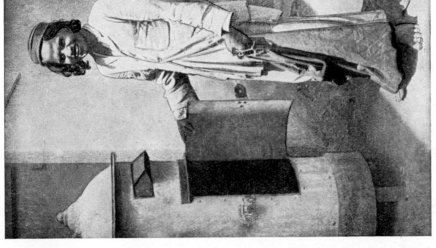

"THE NEXT COLLECTION WILL BE AT——"

A native postman of Mysore about to clear a letter-box.

Photo Exclusive News Agency

KING GEORGE SPEAKING TO THE EMPIRE ON CHRISTMAS DAY

Photo Central Press

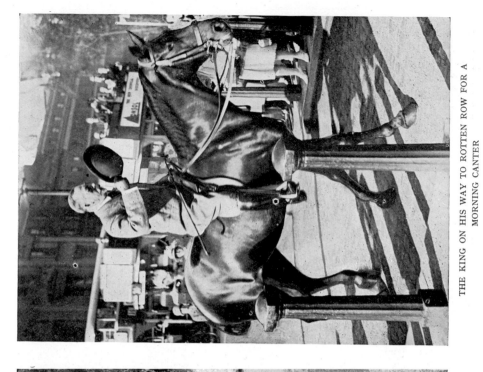

THE KING ON HIS WAY TO ROTTEN ROW FOR A
MORNING CANTER

Fox Photo

THE KING AND QUEEN AT BOGNOR REGIS DURING HIS
MAJESTY'S CONVALESCENCE IN 1929

Photo Central Press

IV

THE KING AND HIS PEOPLE

WHEN we look back at the long pageant of English kings wending its way through the history-books, we see Angevins and Plantagenets, Tudors, and Stuarts, and Georges as remote, magnificent figures, set against a background of memorable events. Those far-off monarchs were probably quite human, simple, and ordinary in their everyday lives, and some of them were charming and kindly as well ; but to their subjects they must have seemed almost as gorgeously remote as they do to us.

The modern point of view is different—as different as our modern clothes are from the gaily-hued garments of the past, or our modern steamers from the little square-sailed cockle-shells of the first English explorers. We feel that our King is one of ourselves, that he and his Queen and their children and grand-children belong to us, and that their doings concern us almost as much as our own. When King Edward VII died, it was said that he was a person of whom his humbler subjects spoke as if he were a sort of prosperous elder brother ; and to this generation it sometimes must seem as if King George were a sort of important and yet sympathetic uncle. This is something new in the history of kingship ; some of the old barriers are being knocked away ; but the old foundations are not being weakened in the process. Those foundations were never more solid than in this twenty-fifth year of King George V's reign.

Every biographer of King George comments on his con-scientious work for his people, whose welfare he has so much at heart. This is not a mere empty phrase. Both he and the

Queen interest themselves actively and intelligently in housing, health, and general social problems. Every scheme for the improvement of the conditions under which the workers live has their ready sympathy, and they often devote a great deal of time and trouble to giving that sympathy practical expression. When the history of this reign comes to be written, they will be honoured as Sovereigns who have served their country faithfully, wisely, and well during years as full of difficulties, and even of serious dangers, as any period in England's long chronicle.

The King's Broadcast

The focus-point of the King's contact with his subjects, and of their affection and personal loyalty to him, has centred undoubtedly in his Christmas broadcast messages of the last few years. He speaks alone from one of the smaller sitting-rooms at Sandringham, and the message is clearly heard all over the world. Canada and South Africa cable to say that every sentence comes through distinctly ; Australia and New Zealand listen-in at three o'clock in the morning to hear it, and it is not merely a wonderful feat of scientific skill. Its achievement places the King in a totally new relationship to the Empire, for how many of us, before the days of wireless, had ever heard the King's voice ? Cold print can be very cold indeed, although Royal messages are certainly often good to read. But to hear the actual voice of the man, speaking with intensely personal feeling to each of us in our own homes, is something so poignant and individual, that the King has come far closer to his people through the medium of the spoken word, than ever before seemed possible.

This is what he said, as he entered on his Silver Jubilee year :

> On this Christmas Day I send to all my people everywhere my Christmas greeting. The day with its hallowed memories is the festival of the family.

I should like to think that you who are listening to me now in whatever part of the world you may be, and all the peoples of this Realm and Empire, are bound to me and to one another by the spirit of one great family. . . .

My desire and hope is that the same spirit may become even stronger in its hold and wider in its range. The world is still restless and troubled. The clouds are lifting, but we have still our own anxieties to meet.

I am convinced that if we meet them in the spirit of one family we shall overcome them, for then private and party interests will be controlled by care for the whole community.

It is as members of one family that we shall to-day, and always, remember those other members of it who are suffering from sickness or from lack of work and hope ; and we shall be ready to do our utmost to befriend them.

I send a special greeting to the peoples of my Dominions overseas. Through them the family has become a fellowship of free nations, and they have carried into their own homes the memories and traditions of the Mother Country. With them I bear in my heart to-day the peoples of my far-distant Colonies. The bond of the one spirit knows no barriers of space. . . .

May I add very simply and sincerely that if I may be regarded as in some true sense the head of this great widespread family, sharing its life and sustained by its affection, this will be a full reward for the long and sometimes anxious labours of my reign of well nigh five and twenty years. . . .

For you all, and especially for your children, I wish a happy Christmas. I commend you to "the Father of Whom every family in heaven and on earth is named."

God bless you all.

The King's Illness

When, on a day in late November 1928, it was announced that the King was suffering from a cold " with some fever," there was little apprehension. It was known that he had caught a chill out shooting in the rain at Sandringham, but inquiries at the Palace elicited reassuring answers. The next day, however, there were grave headlines in the papers, with the news that a third doctor had been called in, and that congestion of the lungs was feared.

Overseas

The King knows the Empire well. He went on his first world-tour when a midshipman in the *Bacchante*, as we shall see in another chapter, and then, as Duke of Cornwall, in 1901 voyaged in the *Ophir* to Australia for the State Opening of the Commonwealth Parliament. Thence he and the Duchess, as she then was, went to New Zealand, and so home by Mauritius, South Africa, and Canada.

As Prince of Wales he went to India and Burma in 1905, and again as King in 1911, the first occasion on which a British king was to be attended by a Ruling Chief-in-Waiting, the Maharajah of Udaipur. Sir Pertab Singh was in the royal retinue, and only a few years later led his troops in the King-Emperor's cause in the European War.

A glittering and gorgeous Durbar was held at Delhi, where the painted State elephants of the ruling princes made a brave show; and the King and Queen together laid the foundation-stones of the new capital city of India.

The King has a very practical knowledge of what concerns his people in the Overseas Dominions. When Mr Ferguson, the Premier of Ontario, came to England some years ago, he said that the King was the best-informed man on Canadian affairs that he had met in England. He added: "His Majesty has the peculiar problems and features of each province well in mind. Just think of the King knowing about power-developments in Ontario and Quebec, and being able to compare them with the costs of development here, where they have to burn coal to generate electricity! His Majesty talked of South African, New Zealand, and Australian affairs; he showed an intense knowledge of every part of the Empire, and it is quite obvious that he is a close student of world affairs, especially of Empire affairs."

It is worth quoting Mr Ferguson's remarks in full, as he sums up the King's attitude to the Dominions from his own first-hand impressions.

The King sent a message not long ago to his Eskimo subjects in Labrador, carried to them by the Governor of the Hudson Bay Company who went out from England on a tour of inspection. The message ran as follows :

> The Message of King George, who rules the British Empire, and of Queen Mary, his Wife, to the Innuit.
>
> The Queen and I send to our loyal Innuit subjects, who dwell throughout Northern Canada and on the shores of Labrador, a message of Greeting from our home in the great encampment of London. In every part of the British Empire, be it ever so many sleeps from our encampment, the happiness of our subjects deeply affects the personal happiness of the Queen and myself.
>
> You should know that we have often heard tell that no people are merrier, more friendly, or more thoughtful for their families than the Innuit. In the same way that parents are proud of their children so the Queen and I take especial pride in our faithful and hardy Innuit.
>
> May each Innuit family thrive, and may your children and grand-children learn in their turn to do honour alike to their parents and to the British Empire.

This delightful message shows the amazingly human interest the King takes in all his people, from such great events as the opening of the Australian Federal Parliament at Canberra, to the family affairs of his ' merry Innuit ' or Eskimos.

It is far cry from the ice-fields of Labrador to that small group of Islands in the English Channel which are the sole survivors of the King's ancient Duchy of Normandy. King John, who lost most of the French possessions of the English Crown, held to his Islands. He visited them twice to encourage the islanders to repel French invasion, and granted them the privilege of self-government, so that they should have no direct link with the administration of the Duchy.

Equally ancient is the privilege of the island militia, which

is exempt to this day from all military service out of its particular
island, except under the personal command of their ' Duke,' or
in an effort to reconquer England should it revolt against him !

Some years ago when King George of England, or Duke of
Normandy, as the people of the Channel Islands love to call him,
visited his Norman domain, many curious customs were revived
to do him honour. In 1247, King Henry I granted the fief of
Rosel in Jersey, according to old feudal tenure, to one Dreux de
Barentin. A hundred years later his nephew William held the
manor, and as the ancient law ran—" should our lord the King
land in the Island, the said William is bound to go on horseback
into the sea to meet him, until it shall touch the girths of his
horse, and in the same manner he should attend him on his
departure."

Mindful of this ancient command the Seigneur of the Fief
de Rosel would most certainly have complied with tradition, as
his predecessor had done on the last occasion of a similar landing in
the reign of Charles I, but King George, owing to the state of the
tide, landed at the harbour slip, rendering the ' riding into the
sea ' impossible. The Seigneur, none the less, fulfilled his obliga-
tions as best he could, standing with one foot in the water to hand
his Majesty ashore. Being also the King's Butler while he was in
the island, the Seigneur of Rosel accompanied him on his tour,
handed him his tea, and looked after him at luncheon. The
Seigneur de la Trinité, who owed two mallards to the Duke on his
arrival in Jersey, presented the birds on a silver dish, with gilded
beaks and all their feathers on ; they were afterwards sent on
board the Royal Yacht.

The Seigneurs of both Guernsey and Jersey, who owed direct
homage to the King, owned their allegiance in true feudal fashion.
The senior Seigneurs knelt before the King, placing their hands
in his, and all repeated the old Norman formula : " *Sire, je suis
votre homme liege à vous porter foy et hommage contre tous.*"

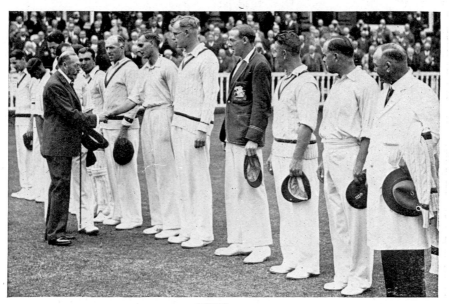

LORDS, 1934
The King with the English team at the Second Test Match between England and Australia.
Photo Sport and General

WEMBLEY, 1934
The King at the Cup Final, with the Manchester City team.
Photo Graphic Photo Union

THE KING AT A CATTLE-SHOW, ADMIRING A PRIZE-WINNER

Photo Central Press

ADMIRING THE PRODUCE OF AN ALLOTMENT GARDEN

Photo Central Press

For this vow of fealty the King sent a formal receipt for " *l'hommage qu'il doit et à cause du franc fief de* (name of fief) *en notre isle de Jersey (or Guernsey) parcelle de notre duché de Normandie.*"

In Guernsey the islanders are pledged to redeem the King should he be put in prison ! No people are more loyal to him than those living in this tide-swept corner of his Dominions, proudly English, yet as proudly upholding their ancient traditions.

In England

We have seen elsewhere in this book that the King's days are far more occupied with routine duties of State than many people suppose, and that he is one of the best-informed men in the country on matters concerning his overseas Dominions and Colonies, and on political and social problems at home. It is amazing that he should find time at all to study conditions, but he began betimes, for when he was a boy on his first voyage, he wrote in his diary, " Few things have struck me more than the absence of all sign of poverty and distress in Australia." The state of the actual living conditions of his people are still the King's sincerest anxiety. He is always urging the need for action in his speeches, and lending his full support to new trade enterprises likely to lead to increased employment.

From his father the King has derived this sympathetic attitude towards social reform. " To build upon the foundation of the past a new order for our common life must be our task for the future. May we preserve, strengthen, and renew those ideals of liberty and freedom for which we have fought ! " So he spoke after the War, and so he feels to-day.

How does the King put precept into practice, so far as he is able ?

He was one of the first to reduce rents on his own property when the slump years came, and to give ground for allotment-holders. People may forget that at that difficult time of national crisis the King voluntarily gave up a very large sum a year from the Privy Purse grant, which entailed real sacrifice of his personal comfort. You may suppose that the King's income is enormous, and that a reduction would make very little difference to him, but long before it ever reaches him the Treasury have deducted hundreds of pounds to pay for salaries, works, repairs, and upkeep of the Royal Households. These sums affect the lives of a great number of individual families who are dependent upon them. It is as if the King were what is sometimes called a Captain of Industry, financing a huge concern out of what he earns, and just as responsible as any industrial owner for the employment of his staffs. In an earlier chapter something has been said about the actual source of the royal revenues.

Consequently the King realizes the need for economy as much as any of his people, and you will find that he seldom visits a town without writing beforehand to the Mayor asking him not to involve the place in any unnecessary expense on his behalf—a thoughtful act that may sometimes pass unnoticed.

The characteristic example of the practical concern of the King and Queen for the country may be found in the British Industries Fair. This has always been of particular interest to them. From small beginnings, as a temporary affair to help traders in war-time when foreign goods were cut off, it has grown to enormous proportions, and last year covered thirty-four acres of land, with a thirty-two mile frontage of stands. The Fair has had its moments of difficulty, but never have its Royal patrons failed to support it, and they have directly helped it to succeed by their personal efforts on its behalf.

The Royal Warrant Holders have lately been brought to the notice of the public, in the news of the presentation to the King,

on the occasion of his Jubilee, of The King's House, to be built
and equipped by them for his own use at Burhill in Surrey.
They are "tradesmen to the Court," and among those who
have the right to use the sign of the Royal Arms above their
doors are still to be found a lamprey pie-maker and a horse-
milliner, the privilege of the latter being to supply rosettes and
ribbons for the decoration of the Royal coaches. They number
fifteen hundred, and have been well called " The Garter Knights
of Commerce."

To tell of the great industrial undertakings to which the King
has given his generous support would fill a book in itself. Our
thoughts at once turn to one of the engineering marvels of the
century—the completion of the Mersey Tunnel—the opening of
which the King attended last year ; to the launch of the
giant Cunarder, the *Queen Mary* ; to the opening of the new
Lloyd's building in the City of London, with all that it stands for
in the world of British commerce ; to that of Ken Wood, as a
place of public enjoyment for the public for ever. Still fresh
in the public memory are the inauguration of the greatest
graving dock in the world at Southampton, and the opening
of University and Library buildings at Manchester and at
Cambridge.

The King's hobbies include agriculture and stock-breeding.
He shows stallions at the Shire Horse Show, sheep at the Smith-
field Club, shorthorn bulls at the Royal Agricultural Hall,
Islington, and cockerels from his Windsor farm at Slough. Many
of his fine beasts are seen sporting the brightly hued rosettes which
mark the prize-winner. He experiments with flax-growing on
his Norfolk estates.

It would be difficult to mention a solitary department of civic
or national activity which has not come within the sphere of
royal influence. Town-dwellers and country-folk, farmers and

merchants, workers in every field, have been encouraged by the King's sympathy and very often helped unconsciously by his quiet collaboration. No single man of our time is able to exert a greater influence over the destinies of so many millions of men, women, and children.

V

THE KING HIMSELF

By

M. C. CAREY

V

THE KING HIMSELF

KING GEORGE is often seen wearing naval uniform, in which he always seems to be most at home, for he is a real sailor who has received the arduous and exacting training of a naval officer. He went to sea when he was a boy of fourteen, just like any other cadet, and served with his elder brother in H.M.S. *Bacchante* when she went for a three years' cruise round the world.

The two brothers were very popular, and were known among the cadets as the Little Sprats, a joke on their father's title of ' Prince of W(h)ales.' Prince George was treated exactly like the other junior officers, and took his turn in going aloft, boat duty, and sail drill, though both Princes had extra work to get through, as they had a tutor on board. In a ship every officer and man has his own duties allotted to him which must be carried out to the letter, and this early training has helped to make the King the hard worker he is, and a man of exemplary punctuality.

Prince George genuinely loved the sea ; it was no mere duty for him to work his way up in the Service, and he stayed in it long enough to command Torpedo Boat 79 as a lieutenant, and later the gunboat *Thrush* on the North American station. A man was once put on board the *Thrush* to be taken to a naval prison to serve a sentence. His fault was not a very grave one, but he had got out of hand, and discipline had to be maintained. The Prince made a point of having a talk with this man, to find out for himself what had gone wrong. On his release, the sailor found he had been transferred to the *Thrush* ; the Prince had another straight talk with him, gave him a sovereign and shore leave, and the man ended up with good rank and his pension. He might never have made good but for the Prince's timely interest and practical help.

The ' Britannia '

It was about this time that the Prince had his first sailing yacht, the *White Rose*, built for him and launched at Cowes. Ever since he had been quite a small boy he had sailed with his father, and when he was nine was in the *Hildegarde* when she won the Queen's Cup at Cowes. So, although he had to give up the sea as a professional sailor when a young man, he never forsook it as a sport.

Every summer he is to be found at Cowes for the regatta, sailing the old *Britannia*, and hoping for half a gale of wind so that she may win her races. Out in all weathers, even since his long illness, the King is recognized by all sportsmen as one after their own hearts, keen to sail a good race, " always ready with a cheer for his more modern rivals, hardest and heartiest of all in a breeze of wind."

Yachtsmen, whether they race big yachts of the *Britannia* class at Cowes or model yachts on the Round Pond, may well give a thought to King George who loves a good race as much as they do, and to King Charles II, who was our first king to make yachting a royal hobby. " Two leagues travel at sea was more pleasure to him than twenty by land," wrote Pepys of his royal master, and before the end of his reign he had fourteen royal yachts, as well as several model yachts, which he used to sail on the ornamental water in St James's Park. King George has no such private fleet and no such toys, but he agrees with King Charles about the sea.

The King was at the wheel when the *Britannia* won her two-hundredth race five years ago. You can imagine the thrill of

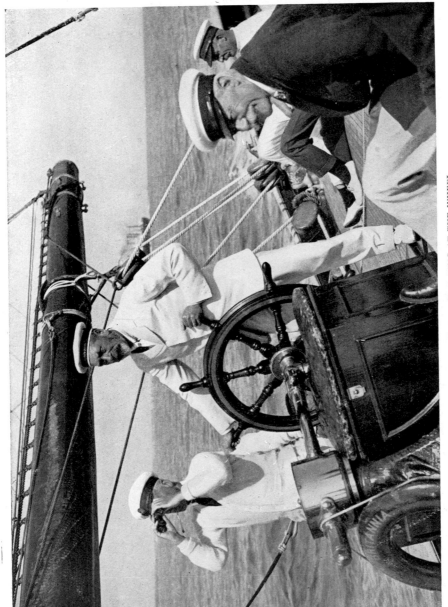

ABOARD THE *BRITANNIA* : THE KING AT THE WHEEL

Photo Central Press

THE *BRITANNIA* OFF COWES

Photo Sport and General

that moment to all on board! Double prize-money was given to the captain and the crew to celebrate the double century of wins, and the King went ashore to receive the delighted congratulations which were showered upon him. Is it to be wondered at that after such marvellous racing days in the old yacht the King should prefer to keep *Britannia*, even though he has been offered the gift of a new 'J' class yacht in honour of his Jubilee?

The Royal Yacht

We cannot leave the sea without a word about the Royal Yacht, the *Victoria and Albert*, which is, as you probably know, a big steam yacht, used by the King and Queen when staying at Cowes or when reviewing the fleet on special occasions.

The 'V. and A.,' as she is known in the fleet, is not as old as the *Britannia*, for she was launched in 1899. Queen Victoria was very much interested in the plans drawn up for her, but did not live to go on board. The yacht is very comfortably furnished; she is designed rather for calm seas and home waters than for long voyages (though the King sailed in her to the Mediterranean), and the royal study on board is furnished as any private room at the Palace might be.

When living on board at Cowes in August, the King begins work at 8 o'clock each morning, and goes through every Foreign Office cable and document that is sent daily to him from Whitehall, as part of his usual routine for the day. He gives infinite attention to everything that is brought to his notice, and his questions are frequent and very much to the point.

The Royal Yacht is always connected by direct undersea telephone to the nearest post office on shore. "Royal Yacht speaking," comes the call, and private business on the line must give way to the probable call to London. The ship is watched by every man-o'-war in company with her, and a signalman is always on duty night and day in each vessel keeping a strict look out for a possible signal from her.

The Queen spends most of her time ashore when the yacht is at Cowes, but the King, when the business of the day is over, loses no time in getting aboard *Britannia,* for he goes to the regatta to sail and not to look on.

The *Victoria and Albert* flies three flags ; the Royal Standard at her main, the King's red and white flag at her fore, and the Union Jack at her mizzen.　These flags, in the language of the sea, say three things.　First, " I am, by the Grace of God, George V, King of England " ; secondly, " I am George, King of England, and the Lord High Admiral of the English Fleet " ; and, thirdly, the Union Jack proclaims " I am the King of Great Britain and Ireland."　Any ship that passes and sees these flags, dips her ensign in salute when she comes abreast.

Racing

After yacht-racing and the sea the King loves his racehorses. There is a friendly wager every year between the manager of the racing stables and the captain of *Britannia* as to whether the yacht will win more races afloat than the royal horses ashore.　Usually *Britannia* wins.

The King won his first classic victory at Newmarket, when his filly Scuttle came home first in the Thousand Guineas.　King Edward won the Derby three times, but King George has not yet been so fortunate as to win it once.　The Royal Stables are at Newmarket, and when the King goes there for the July meeting he usually stays in the bachelor suite at the Jockey Club rooms in the High Street, being treated as a private member without ceremony.

King George was, curiously enough, the first British monarch to attend a Scottish race meeting ; he went to Musselburgh, near Edinburgh, in 1931.

The King has won races with Sport of Kings—a splendidly appropriate name for a royal horse! Limelight was another winner, and The Abbot and Friar Marcus were others.

Shooting

In the opinion of many the King is still the best shot in England, and as a young man he was always very keen on this sport, tramping over miles of heather with his ghillies on the moors round Balmoral or out on the hills after stag. It was a chill caught out shooting that developed into his long and serious illness. On the first of October his keepers send twelve brace of pheasants to Buckingham Palace, and the coverts are not shot over again until the King himself arrives at Sandringham later in the month. A great deal of game is always sent to hospitals by the King in the season.

The Royal Train

When the Court moves from London to Balmoral the King travels on this long journey by special train, and most people think that this train really belongs to him, and that he can use it free of charge. But this is far from the case. Each of the four railway groups keeps a ' special ' at the disposal of the King and Queen, but when it is in use the King pays for it at so much a mile, as well as all the first-class fares for the Household and members of the Royal Suite who are travelling with him. You will notice that the Royal Train is not very often used in consequence, and that the King for the most part travels either by road, if the distance is not too great, or in a royal saloon coach attached to an ordinary train, while others members of the Royal Family just have carriages reserved for them as any other passengers might.

It is strange to think that it is nearly a hundred years since

Queen Victoria went for her first railway journey from Slough
to Paddington, the Prince Consort being, it was said, distinctly
nervous. On that occasion her coachman insisted on travelling
beside the engine-driver, and her Master of the Horse inspected
the engine before it started. There is a story that a certain
Shah of Persia, when visiting England, was brought by train
from Dover to London faster than the ten miles an hour limit
which he considered safe. He was so angry about this that on
reaching Victoria he demanded the instant execution of the
driver !

Nowadays the Royal Train does not even have a special pilot-
engine running ahead to see that the line is clear, nor are there
look-out men all along the line as there were in the old Queen's
day. Some time before the train is due to pass, the gates at
level crossings are locked, and for half an hour ahead shunting
operations stop on that part of the line. Four sharp rings,
repeated three times, is the signal that announces that the
Royal Train is approaching. The Royal Arms are fixed in front
of the engine, and not so very long ago it was the custom to
whitewash the top layer of coal in the tender.

On board the train is a special staff of telephone and telegraph
operators ; if at any time the train comes to a standstill, they are
able to tap the telegraph wires alongside the line, and so get
into touch with the nearest signal box.

The Royal Saloon has a desk in it, and is fitted up as a study,
so that the King's correspondence can be dealt with while he is
travelling, for he cannot afford to let his letters accumulate. In
each of the compartments in the Royal Coach there is a bell
marked ' Equerry,' so that the King can get into touch immediately with the equerry on duty, who carries about an electric
bell with him, and plugs it into the wall wherever he may be
sitting.

Daily Life

The King is one of the busiest men in the country ; there is no question of a five-day week for him. One must not think of him as only driving about to attend functions and open Parliament, though his days are mapped out months ahead with public engagements that he never fails to keep, and if " punctuality is the politeness of kings," many of his subjects have much to learn from their Sovereign.

There is probably no better informed man in the country to-day than the King, standing as he does above party politics, yet intensely interested in everything that affects the welfare of the country both at home and abroad. The fact that his advice is so often sought by his Ministers shows how high they rank him as a statesmen.

When in London the King usually works before breakfast, for he has an enormous amount to get through each day. Possibly there may be sixty or seventy letters by the first post, the most important of which go to him direct.

Directly after breakfast he goes to his study, and his Private Secretary brings him another batch of State papers and correspondence ; red Government boxes begin to arrive, and the papers are considered and signed, and probably there may be a number of officers' commissions in the Navy, Army, or Air Force, all of which must bear the King's signature.

Audiences are granted to Cabinet Ministers, Government officials, Colonial Governors, Ambassadors, and many other people of importance throughout the morning, while meetings of the Privy Council, Investitures, and Levees have to be fitted into the week's programme. It is no wonder that the King is constantly to be found at work again in the afternoon, when he is not carrying out some public engagement, and he usually returns to his study in the evening. His Secretaries are in constant attendance, and one is always on duty. Even when the King is out of London he keeps in the closest touch by telephone, and his work goes on just the same.

The King's Own Post Office

The King has his own Post Office and Court Postmaster. Tucked away in a corner of Buckingham Palace is a large room where the Court Postmaster and his staff will be dealing at the time of the Jubilee with hundreds of letters and telegrams of congratulation, with numbers of parcels from the King's and Queen's personal friends, and with countless telephone calls on the private telephone exchange.

The King's and Queen's birthdays bring hundreds of telegrams which their Majesties like to see and answer, and when the Duke of Kent married Princess Marina as many as 1614 telegrams from all sorts of people were sent to them, and every one was answered. The Court Post Office had to transmit over 3600 telegrams in all.

Wherever the King goes the Court Postmaster goes with him and opens up a Court Post Office. There is one at Windsor Castle, others at Sandringham and Balmoral, and there is even one on board the Royal Yacht *Victoria and Albert* and on the Royal Train when it stops for one night with the King on board.

When the King is away from London all Government Office dispatch-boxes, as well as letters for his Majesty and for anyone staying with him, are placed in special bags, which are chained up and padlocked and sent direct through the post to wherever the King is—except, however, to Windsor, where, so important is the dispatch, that it is sent by motor mail-van from Buckingham Palace to the Castle and back again. On board the Royal Yacht sailors are the postmen. Sometimes a very special dispatch-box or letter has to be sent to the King ; then a special messenger travels with it as quickly as possible.

Special bags are also made up for the Royal Princes when they are travelling abroad. For this purpose the Air Mail is nearly always used. You will remember that the King sent the first Air Mail letter to Australia and got the first Australian Air Mail letter back.

The King's telegrams come from all parts of the world to the Central Telegraph Office in London, and then to Buckingham Palace over an instrument called a teleprinter—that is, a telegraph printer. They are sent and received on a machine like a typewriter, and messages typed out at one end are printed like a telegram at the other. A few years ago, when the Prince of Wales was in Buenos Aires attending the Trade Exhibition, messages came through by cable direct to the Palace. A teleprinter was not used then, but what is known as a ' siphon recorder ' transmitted the telegrams ; messages came out in long, wavy, up-and-down lines on the paper, and these had to be turned into ordinary words, as Morse Code is decoded into letters.

Telephone work at Court Post Offices is very important. Two operators are hard at work during the morning, and one during the rest of the day. These two are very skilled men, and go away with the King to most places. There is an operator on duty all through the night ; it is important that the King should be in touch with the outside world at all times.

Conversations are held with people everywhere, even as far away as New Zealand, Australia, South Africa, Canada, and South America. In the Royal Yacht, too, talks take place all day long through a special cable under the sea connected to Buckingham Palace and elsewhere.

On the private exchange at the Palace there are 120 short lines to various rooms of the Private Secretaries and other persons, as well as lines to St James's Palace, Windsor Castle, and Government Offices. The operators are continually watching little flash-lamps, which glow when anyone rings up. They can always tell when the King wants to speak—a tiny red lamp lights up. When the Private Secretaries and other important people ring up, a bright green lamp glows ; less important people have white lamps. All the Court Post Office exchanges are secret ones, and even the operators cannot listen in.

Pets

But what of the man himself when the day's work is over, and when, for an hour or two, he allows himself to relax in the privacy of his own home ? Is he always hedged about with etiquette and formality ?

Charlotte, his grey parrot, would answer ' No ' if she heard that question, for she is the King's constant companion, and sits on his shoulder as he walks about the Palace garden, as she did long ago when, as a young naval officer, he bought her at Port Said. He is devoted to Charlotte ; she goes with him wherever the Court moves—to Sandringham, to Balmoral, or even to Eastbourne on his recent short holiday. Usually she spends the day in his study on her perch. She is not much of a talker, but the King makes the greatest pet of her, and has been known to telephone from London to Balmoral when she was once left there for a short time, entirely to ask after Charlotte's health !

Bob, the Cairn terrier, does not understand formality either where his master is concerned. He also goes for walks with him in the garden, and is the most friendly little dog. And the lovely birds in the aviary at Newmarket, blue budgerigars and the rare scarlet-chested parakeet, are not awed by royalty, but chirp and chatter when the King visits them.

The Stamp-Collection

Most of us collect something or other, and many of us collect stamps. It brings the King very close to us to know that he owns one of the most famous stamp-collections in the world. A

THE KING LOOKING AT ONE OF HIS RACEHORSES AT NEWBURY

Photo Sport and General

"OUT WITH THE GUNS" AT BALMORAL

Photo Central Press

THE KING TIGER-SHOOTING IN NEPAL

Photo Central Press

THE KING AND QUEEN AT THE ROYAL HORTICULTURAL SOCIETY'S SHOW

Fox Photos

whole room at Buckingham Palace is given up to the two hundred leather-bound volumes, which are in the charge of a distinguished expert. The King collects stamps of the Empire only. The most valuable one in the collection came from Mauritius, and it is worth any amount of money. It is a very rare issue, dating from the days when Mauritius stamps were stamped singly with a hand-die. In the collection is also that rare fourpenny Western Australian, with the swan upside down, and the fourpenny of the same kind with the word ' Australia ' in half-size letters.

The King began to collect when he was a midshipman, and it is his real hobby. When, during the Great War, he was going through much mental strain and anxiety, it was to his collection that he turned for moments of distraction, and he would often be found in his stamp-room upstairs poring over some rare specimen with a magnifying-glass.

The King's Homes and Home Life

Though it is from St James's Palace that Royal Proclamations are dated and within the dusky brick walls of the old Tudor hunting-box that Royal Levees are held, the King when in London lives at Buckingham Palace and not at St James's.

The original house was built in 1703 for John Sheffield, Duke of Buckingham—hence its name—and was purchased by George III, in whose days it was known as the Queen's House. Since then it has been three times altered and enlarged. The simple but dignified frontage added in 1913 is familiar to all Londoners, who, as they approach it from the long, tree-fringed avenue of the Mall, can tell at a glance whether the King is in residence or not. The Royal Standard flies from the Palace flagstaff when the King is staying there ; when he is absent, it is replaced by the Union Jack.

The most ancient and historic home of the Kings of England is Windsor Castle, the great grey fortress-palace sprawling like a watchful dragon on the hill above the green playing-fields of Eton. William the Conqueror built a stronghold here, on the site of an Anglo-Saxon one, and the Round Tower dates from the time of Henry III. The castle, surrounded by a park of eighteen hundred acres planted with fine timber and stocked with fallow deer, contains within its walls the lovely chapel of St George, sacred to the Most Noble Order of the Garter, of which the Sovereign is the head.

Beautiful though Windsor certainly is, there is about it an atmosphere of stateliness and ceremony from which royal princes must sometimes be glad to escape. The King has two such ways of escape, two homes where the outer trappings of royal pomp may for a time be laid aside, though the daily routine of royal responsibility still goes on.

One of these is the manor of Sandringham in Norfolk, a red brick house of Elizabethan design, built by King Edward. When the present King was first married, he and the Duchess of York lived at York Cottage, a smaller house in the grounds, and there several of their children were born.

" I hope you will like Sandringham," said the King once to a newly-joined member of the Royal Household, " *I* do." At Sandringham he lives the life of an English squire, interested in his garden, his farms, and his tenants, and taking an active share in the life of the village.

In Scotland the Royal Family have their fourth home, Balmoral Castle, in the valley of the Dee, nine hundred feet above sea-level. The house was rebuilt by Queen Victoria in what is called the ' Scottish baronial ' style of architecture, with many little bastions and turrets. Here the King goes every autumn to shoot over the wide grouse-moors.

The King leads the simplest of lives. He seldom dines out, and in everyday life dispenses with much formality. He does not care for cards or billiards, smokes chiefly cigarettes, and lives much in his study, meeting the Queen at meals to discuss the events of the day. The Queen never fails to be at home to give the King his tea if she knows that he will be in at that hour ; and this gives their Majesties an opportunity to discuss the events of the day and the plans of the morrow.

When guests are not being entertained, both the King and the Queen go early to bed ; dinner is usually at 8.30, and the King goes to read or work in his study afterwards, and the Queen to her sitting-room. He is a great reader of history and biography, though not of novels. Books such as those describing the climbing of Mount Everest or those dealing with exploration and adventure, appeal to him particularly, and whether it is the thrill of a hard-fought game or a daring record-breaking exploit, the King takes a keen interest in it, or in anything that tests a man's skill and physical endurance. He is blessed with the faculty of keeping a sort of mental card-index of what he reads, and in common with many royal personages he has a truly remarkable memory, not only for faces, but also for the spoken word. He forgets nothing that he has once been told, and if a statement made to him errs on the side of inaccuracy the speaker may be fairly sure that eventually his error will be brought home to him.

The King is always perfectly dressed ; not necessarily in the latest fashion but turned out correctly for every occasion, his trousers marvellously creased, always down the side, not the front. Every day when the Court is at Buckingham Palace a button-hole is sent up to him from Windsor, and a bunch of violets for the Queen from the conservatories or gardens.

His grandchildren, of whom he has four, are the greatest joy to the King. The two little princesses are reputed to be able to twist him round their fingers. They are devoted to him, and are in very little awe of 'Grandpa,' whom they visit constantly at Sandringham for weeks at a time. But that is not to say that their manners are not of the most perfect, for they are extremely strictly brought up. The two little Princesses come down to see their grandparents after luncheon or after tea ; their nurse opens the door, and they run in. Each makes her little curtsey, then hurries across the room to kiss first the King's hand and then his cheek, before beginning to play. The King's two grandsons, the children of his only daughter, the Princess Royal, are, like him, keen sportsmen.

Few people realize the essential simplicity of this very great gentleman who rules over the Empire, a man who rather than disappoint a rally of Boy Scouts took the place of the Duke of York at the last moment so as ' not to let the boys down ' ; who told a little girl, on giving her a Bible as her school prize, that his grandmother, Queen Victoria, had once given him a Bible on his birthday and told him to read it every day, and added, " I cannot perhaps expect you to do this, but I have always done so " ; and a man who, when speaking to the boys on board the training ship *Worcester*, gave them this message :

> There are perhaps two points that I think you should keep before you as guiding principles :
> I should say above all things—be loyal.
> And the other is—be thorough.
> Whatever you do, do it as well as you can, and put your whole heart and soul into that work.

This is the charge given to the boys and girls of England by one who has never failed to live up to it himself.